Bootlegging Adventures in Northwest Montana

By
Darris Flanagan

All Rights Reserved
Copyright @2023 by Darris Flanagan

Table of Contents

Preface	5-6
Introduction	7-8
What Was Prohibition?	9
What Led To Prohibition?	10-11
All Nations Welcome But Carrie	11-12
Prohibition Was Popular	12-14
Bootlegging, Rumrunning, Moonshine	14-15
Moonshine	15-17
Moonshine Recipe By Sid Workman	18-19
Moonshine Dangers	20-24
Too High A Price	24-26
Tobacco Valley Moonshining	27-28
Moonshine As Medicine	28-29
Speakeasies	29-31
How To Be A Successful Bootlegger	31-32
Rumrunners	32-34
How A Hijacking Gang Operated	34
A Rumrunner Death And Hijacking	35
Even The Streets Of Town Were Unsafe!	35-36
Everyone Was Bribed	36-39
Smuggling In Canadian Booze	39-41
Rumrunners' Cars	41-45
Most Rumrunners Escape	45
Charles L. Sheridan	46
Coal Trains	47-49
Other Choices For Smuggling Across The Border	49-51
Booze Smugglers Take To The Air	52-53
Why Own When You Can Steal	53
Information Pipeline	54
Roosville and Gateway	54-58
Rumrunning Began Slow	59
Get Set Go	60-62
Woman Bootleggers	63-64

Blow The Whistle For A Quart	64-65
A Hot Bottle Works Fine	65-66
Whispering Willy Watkins Salesman And Bootlegger	66-67
Whispering Willy Arrested	67-68
Overnight Felons	69
Dry Squads	70-71
Another View of Montana Enforcement	71-73
Authorities Work Together	73
The Honest Bootlegger	74
Here Piggy, Piggy: It's Not Always Booze	75
It Takes One to Know One!	75-76
Making Inroads	76-77
Northwest Montana Treated Unfairly By Raids	77-80
Rumrunner, Saloon Owner and Criminal	80-81
The Truth Or Not	82
Stryker – Radnor – Olney: A Place To Get Caught	83-86
A True Amateur	86-87
Lucky It Was A Thumb	87-88
Was It The Same Jane?	88
He's All Man	89-90
Sheriff Baney As An Enforcer	91-93
Stop! Stop In the Name of the Law	93-94
Dry Squad Stops The Sheriff	95
The Dry Squad Found Nothing	95-97
Montana Victims of Prohibition Enforcement	97-100
The Danger Of Being A Prohibition Agent	100-103
Ambushed By Dry Agents At Roosville	103-105
Punishment For Prohibition Crimes	106
Moonshiners And Rumrunners In Jail	107-108
Montana Quits Enforcement	109-111
Federal Agents Continue The Losing Battle	111-112
The End Was Coming	112-114
Can You Believe The Government's Poisoning Plan?	114-117

Now You Can Drink Beer	118-119
An Amendment Needed To Repeal An Amendment	119-120
Montana Was In No Hurry!	120-121
Results Of Prohibition	121-122
Rumrunners Caches Found Years Later	122
The Cost Of Prohibition In Dollars	123
Some Still Have Prohibition Today	123
NASCAR	124-125
The Final	126
Sources	126-128

Preface

My friend Gary Montgomery wrote a fiction book *Doughboys, Rumrunners and Bootleggers* and when someone asked me a question about rumrunning, I knew a little, but was inspired to learn more. My research made me remember the great times we had as kids as we galloped around the ranch in my brother's Model A. We went through the fields and woods laughing and screaming in fun. I knew then what it must have been like in some ways as a rumrunner racing from the cops. Of course, we weren't being shot at! But what fun we had.

I always write on a subject no one else has. After finishing my last book, I thought that would be my last one. Suddenly I had a topic for a book. I started by rereading a book I enjoyed years before. It was a book about bootlegging which included Northwest Montana. I read *Rum Road to Spokane* and placed it in my library where it sat for forty or more years. Rereading the book, I was addicted to the subject. My research revealed how significant Northwest Montana was to Prohibition enforcement. The two Tobacco Valley history books mention practically nothing about Prohibition which is the same for Whitefish and Kalispell histories forcing me to search elsewhere for stories.

My most important source became the local Eureka paper. I owe a special thanks to librarians Siri Larsen at the Lincoln County Library in Eureka and Amanda Anderson at the Lincoln County High School Library who allowed me access to the Eureka Journals from the 1920s. Without this paper this book could not have been written! I must confess quotes from newspapers are not always word for word. There are slight changes to make them more readable.

As a writer you quickly realize that you depend on many people. There are those who answer phone calls, most I never met and probably never will. Included in this group is almost every museum in Western Montana who were called in an attempt to find stories and photos for this book. The only one I didn't hear from was the Montana Historical Society which didn't answer my email. I had used many of their photos in the past, but they are in the process of construction of a new building. The one thing I learned was Prohibition pictures are few and far between.

Gary Montgomery, a fellow writer, helped me in many ways, some he realizes, and some are from research he has done. Several of the photos in this book are from him. I need to thank my niece, Cathy Kucera and her husband J.J., who answers and fixes all my computer problems, and my proofreader, Susan Ennenbach, who for years has made my writing "readable." When you find a mistake rest assured that it is a result of a change I made after Susan did her work! A big thank-you to Stefnie Peters, who through her magic produces a finished product from my writing and pictures. She does a wonderful job! There are many who help who may never know how they aided me. A necessity thank you goes to all the businesses who sell my books and most especially you the reader. Thanks one and all.

Introduction

When Prohibition is capitalized, it refers to a time in the United States (1920-1933) when the manufacture and sale of alcohol were forbidden by law. Prohibition comes the from the Latin verb prohibere meaning to 'keep in check." Looking back one hundred years, one realizes nothing was kept in check! The Prohibition Era is a part of our history that was never recorded. What an exciting time it must have been, particularly in the Tobacco Valley of Northwest Montana.

Most people went on about their business during Prohibition, but in Eureka when the lumber Mill's planer burned in 1923 and the mill closed for good a few months later there were no jobs. People tried to hold on but over the next ten years that Prohibition lasted over half the residents of the valley left. Beryl Holgren one of the few who wrote about these bootlegging days summed up how everyone was affected. *"Almost everyone who dared got into it, respectable businessmen, the less scrupulous, and those in between."*

Becoming a bootlegger was an opportunity residents turned to, joining the many from outside the area. People were reluctant to talk about the part their families may have had as a bootlegger, moonshiner, or rumrunner or one who aided them. Being involved or knowing those involved meant an obligation to remain discreet. John Leonard told me how shocked he was to learn that his grandfather and his brother were rumrunners. Even fifty years after Prohibition, people were reluctant to talk about their own family's experiences or even tell the names of friends who may have been involved. Now those stories are lost! But others remained, which is the basis of this book. A special thanks to those who related family stories. I know there are more stories out there and I would like to hear them!

This is a collection of articles from newspapers, family stories, memories from oral histories and books. Some are sad, others are humorous, unbelievable, emotional, or happy. This book is the story of car chases on moonlight nights, but darker nights were even better! Moonshine stills were everywhere just waiting for a law officer to find and destroy them. Gun battles and car pursuits led to adventure after adventure. I hope this inspires you to come along and imagine the memories of those days.

[Please note that there are two spellings of whiskey or whisky in this book. To make a long explanation short, whiskey (with an 'e') refers to grain spirits distilled in the United States. Whisky (with no 'e') refers to Canadian spirits. Also note that Rum-runner should technically have a hyphen in the word but most do not use one; so I chose not to.]

What Was Prohibition?

Prohibition became the law of the land in 1920 but began a year earlier in Montana. Nationally the 18th Amendment to the U.S. Constitution banned the manufacture, transportation, and sale of intoxicating liquors. It was ratified in 1919 and was to go into effect a year later. In October 1919, Congress put forth the National Prohibition Act, which provided guidelines for the federal enforcement of Prohibition. Championed by Representative Andrew Volstead of Minnesota, the chairman of the House Judiciary Committee, the legislation is more commonly known as the Volstead Act. As of midnight on January 17, 1920, it became illegal to transport, buy, or sell liquor, but not to drink alcohol. Imagine the scramble to purchase every bottle in sight before midnight!

This is a front page cartoon of the Daily Interlake 1-16-1920. John Barleycorn is a personification of barley as used in any intoxicating liquor.

What Led To Prohibition?

The idea for Prohibition dates to the early 1800s when a wave of religious revivalism swept the United States. Part of this movement called for temperance. In 1838 Massachusetts passed a sobriety law banning the sale of spirits in less than 15-gallon quantities; the law was repealed two years later, but it set a precedent for such legislation. Maine passed the first state Prohibition laws in 1846, followed by a stricter law in 1851.

By the turn of the century, temperance societies like the Woman's Christian Temperance Union (WCTU) were a common fixture in communities across the United States. The Montana chapter was founded in 1883 and was a popular, well-organized women's club focused on reducing the consumption of alcohol in the state. WCTU was very strong in Montana and the Tobacco Valley where they held weekly meetings. Women played a strong role in the temperance movement because alcohol was seen as a destructive force in families and marriages. Today, they continue their work to educate people about the dangers of alcohol and other drug use. The WCTU works to protect families from all negative influences under its "Do Everything" policy. They are the oldest, continuous woman's organization in the world. On the world level, the WCTU was nominated for the Nobel Peace Prize in 2017.

Woman's Christian Temperance Union Symbol

In 1906 a new organization, the Anti-Saloon League, began another wave of attacks on the sale of liquor. The movement was driven by a reaction to urban growth and the rise of evangelical Christianity and its view of saloon culture as corrupt and ungodly. In addition, many factory owners supported Prohibition in their desire to prevent accidents and increase the efficiency of workers in a time of increased industrial production and extended working hours.

All Nations Welcome But Carrie

Eureka and other western Montana cities had a visit in the spring of 1910 from Carry Nation, a nationally known temperance agitator. In 1900 she began a campaign for which she became legendarily known. Supported by "visions" of her divinely inspired mission, her activities became increasingly violent in Kansas. In Wichita she wrecked hotels and other expensive saloons, smashing mirrors, windows, bars, paneling, nude paintings, and valuable liquor stocks. It was also in Wichita that she first used the hatchet which became her distinctive weapon. As Nation's anti-alcohol activities became widely known,

Carrie Nation in 1910 shortly before her death

many bars had this slogan "All Nations Welcome but Carrie." Carrie Nation's (her correct name is Carry Amelia Moor Nation) visit to Eureka was tame by comparison, but it was still controversial. [Flanagan]

Prohibition Was Popular

Temperance advocates promised that National Prohibition would usher in a beautiful new world. Crime, poverty, violence, marital abuse, industrial injuries, sickness, and premature death would all go down. In their place would be prosperity, less violence, fewer injuries, better health, and greater longevity. Deaths during Prohibition were to drop!

In 1917, after the United States entered World War One, President Wilson instituted a temporary wartime prohibition of manufacturing whiskey to save grain for producing food. In August 1917, the Food and Fuel Control Act outlawed the use of any grains or foodstuffs for producing distilled spirits. This emergency wartime measure was set to expire at the end of World War I. Wilson's prohibition had little effect because there was enough whiskey already manufactured to supply consumers for three years and people could make their own. Whisky was being withdrawn from government bonded warehouses at the rate of over 1,000,000 gallons a day. [Eureka Journal 8-30-1917]

Also, in 1917 Congress submitted the 18th Amendment for approval. For an amendment to become part of the constitution three-fourths of the states must approve it, which they did in just 11 months. The amendment was ratified on January 16, 1919, and would go into effect one year later

Might as well get on the wagon, too!
Anaconda Standard

to the day January 17, 1920, at midnight.

There was widespread support for Prohibition when it began. In fact, many states already had state-wide Prohibition before 1920. It went into effect in Idaho and Washington in 1916 and immediately rumrunners began bringing liquor from Montana into those states. There was a particular booze rush before Montana went dry. Following a vote in 1916, Montana was to go dry on July 1, 1919. The statewide vote was 58 percent to 42 for Prohibition. The center of the Prohibition enforcement for western Montana was Lincoln County where voters also favored Prohibition by a slightly higher margin of 60 to 40 percent.

Kenneth Davis in an autobiographical sketch wrote how his dad spent the night before Montana's Prohibition. *In 1919 Prohibition was voted in. One of Dad's jobs as auctioneer was to auction off all the booze in the Eureka saloons. I can remember hanging around the streets on the last evening until way past my bedtime as he went from one bar to the other and auctioned off everything. One of his methods of payment for that was to receive some of the open bottles that were left over. For years he had a whole closet full of very unusual types of exotic liquors and liqueurs such as Rock Candy Whiskey, Applejack, Amaretto, and Triple Sec which I surreptitiously enjoyed a sip at a time until I was discovered in the act.*

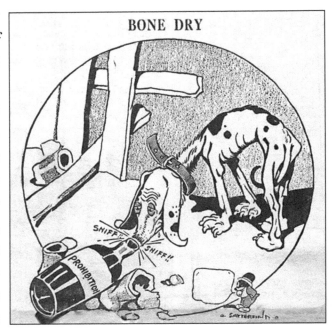

Bootlegging, Rumrunning, Moonshine

There are three principal terms connected to Prohibition. Rumrunning and bootlegging were the illegal smuggling of alcoholic beverages in an area where transportation was forbidden by law. The term rumrunning was at first commonly applied to smuggling over water while bootlegging was applied to smuggling over land, now they are interchangeable. Moonshine was liquor that was produced illegally. The term bootlegging began to have been used in the 1850s to denote the practice of concealing flasks of liquor in boot tops while trading with Native Americans which was illegal. Bootlegging is sometimes used as a term for the whole process and is commonly used for either rumrunning or moonshine. One can almost separate moonshiners and rumrunners into two categories amateur and professional. In Montana moonshine liquor was made everywhere. Rumrunning was busiest at the border. In Northwest Montana it was centralized in the Eureka area. On the plains of Montana rumrunners had many choices for crossing the border. In the Tobacco Valley topography basically restricted smuggling to an area from the Kootenai River to the Galton Mountain Range to the east.

Moonshine

The name moonshine is derived from a tradition of creating alcohol at nighttime, thereby avoiding detection, although the aroma of the process led some law officers directly to a still. Moonshiners distilled their own brews that ranged from excellent to downright deadly. "Bottle men" would hike down the mountain trails, paths, or streets carrying suitcases loaded with booze bound for cities and towns big and small.

Moonshine, also known as "hooch" or "homebrew," was made in stills which changed mash into liquor. Because alcohol has a lower boiling point than water, a still separates the two by heating. The evaporation when it cools is the liquor. A basic still consists of four components. A pot, which is filled with the fermented mash, a heating element which heats the pot from below, a condenser, sometimes water-cooled, which turns the evaporated alcohol back into a liquid and a collection vessel, into which the alcohol flows after it passes through the condenser. Because the process can take a lot of water, stills were often found near a stream. Grocery and hardware stores legally sold a laundry list of what moonshiners needed.

Mash is some combination of water, grain, yeast, and sugar that is allowed to ferment before being distilled into alcohol. Moonshine can be made from any grain or fruit, but most common was corn. Corn or corn meal was often preferred both because of its abundance and because it was a good source of fermentable sugar. Sometimes other ingredients were included to add

A simple still that might be used in a house.

flavor or give a kick. When made with a grain the drink was whiskey, when made with fruit the resulting drink was brandy. During Prohibition, profit-hungry moonshiners started using white sugar instead of corn meal, producing a cheaper product that was technically rum, not whisky.

What makes moonshine different from the whisky one finds on the shelf at a liquor store? Aside from the obvious differences between something made in a sanitized facility and something made at night in the woods, the primary difference is aging. When whisky comes out of the still, it's so clear it looks like water. Moonshiners bottled it and sold it just like that. Commercial alcohols have an amber or golden color to them because they are aged for years in charred oak barrels. The aging process gives them color and mellows the harsh taste. There's no such mellowing with moonshine, which was why it had such "kick." Moonshine contains a high percentage of alcohol, usually more than 100 proof.

One might be wondering about homebrewed beer and wine — these activities were legal during Prohibition, but only for home consumption. Homebrewing is a different activity from distilling alcohol which was illegal in any amount because it was too easy to make a mistake and create a harmful product. Brewed beer or wine had much less alcohol content.

Where was moonshine distilled? The answer is everywhere. Moonshine was distilled in handmade, ramshackle stills found in the woods or mountains. In Montana many farmers and isolated homesteaders supplemented their meager incomes by making moonshine in stills found in the woods. Prohibition led to new places: attics and basements of private homes. Business buildings and even public buildings concealed moonshine operations.

Moonshine Recipe
By Sid Workman

    25 lbs. corn or other grain
        (oats, barley, potatoes, rice, etc.)
    25 lbs. sugar (the more sugar you use, the stronger
        the finished whiskey)

Stir it all up and put in an oak barrel (30-50 gallon) - it'll eat a hole in anything else (fermentation). Add water - approx. 10 gallons. Add yeast (Fleishman's) Beat yeast and water in a cup or bowl and add to the corn/water mixture. Place where warm - between 65 and 75 degrees - and the fermenting will start (you can hear it sizzle) and this goes on for a couple of weeks and finally all at once it stops. It'll get all clear on top, otherwise there'd be a big foamy top on it. Now you're ready to put it in the cooker. Put it on the stove and you got all these connections. Now this stuff is boiling - a lot of pressure here. You have to make a connection here (where the copper coil comes out of the cooker) absolutely airtight. Most of the old people just made a dough out of flour and water and they'd wrap it around this connection, and they'd take an old rag and tie it tight and when it starts to get warm it'll bake that and that's the only connection you've got. Then it's got to go in a barrel of water (the copper coil). Say you've got a half a 30 gallon barrel down here and this coil goes around and around on the inside of it up against the outside wall. When you get the steam agoin' it'll start to boil right up and when it comes through the cold water and out onto the bench in one of these open jars then there's your liquor comin' out. You have to get it regulated right so that - the way we did it anyway - you get real fine kindling wood, and you got a wood stove, course there was no propane in those days. Some people did use kerosine stoves you could take out in the brush someplace and in the summertime, nobody could see your smoke and you were pretty well off there. You might get - let's see - out of five gallons you probably get two and a half gallons. And they call 'em singles. That's the first time you go through. And when you test that stuff it'll test about 40 percent - 40 proof, that's what I mean. In order to get the higher proof whiskey you have to pour it back in the cooker and you run it through again and you get up around anywheres from 80, 90, sometimes 100 proof out of that. Course then people water it down to 70, 80 whatever they want. If you didn't want to water it down you could have some pretty strong whiskey there. But, here's another thing, I've seen my dad take oak barrel staves and split them into real fine pieces and put them in the oven - in the cookstove - and those things would turn brown, real brown. So then he'd put them in the can and that gave it kind of an oak flavor.

Well this, this takes about two weeks...for this to ferment. They call it - stop workin', clears right off on top. Course to run that is just one night's work or maybe half of one night cause this thing runs - if you get it to run one quart every ten minutes, you're doing real good. That's about the best you can get out of it.

If you wanted to get into it a little bigger, you could make a 50 gallon barrel and run four or five of these cans (cookers) in one night. Stay up all night and run 'em. You don't need very much fire. Once you get her going just keep everything burning steady and you gauge everything by how much is coming out down here (the cooling coil). [Montgomery]

Moonshine Dangers

The Anaconda Standard, maybe in jest, maybe in seriousness wrote, "they say moonshine makes a fine weekend drink. You drink it on Wednesday and your weekends right there." [1-24-26]

Moonshine stills were frequently made from car parts, especially radiators, which often contained lead soldering and remnants of antifreeze glycol products that contaminated the moonshine by adding toxins to the drink. Many moonshiners made their beverages quickly and carelessly and those leaching toxins made it poisonous. Sometimes the bootlegger himself was killed from explosions. Stills could be highly flammable with the potential to explode during distillation if they were not properly sealed and vented. If there was a leak releasing ethanol gas in the still a single spark could cause an explosion which is one reason most moonshine distilleries were located outside.

While the flammability of the moonshine distillation process was dangerous in and of itself, the health effects of moonshine-methanol consumption pose a far greater threat. Methanol, or methyl alcohol, is a byproduct of the distilling process and was released in the vapors during evaporation and became part of the alcohol. How flammable and dangerous that chemical can be gaged by the fact that methanol is the primary main ingredient in fuel, pesticides, paint thinners, and more.

Thirty thousand people died during Prohibition from poisoned alcohol. No number was found for Montana, but the newspapers are filled with victims: isolated sheepherders, those having a drink in a speakeasy or teenagers having their first drink.

This newspaper article was published soon after Prohibition went into effect in Montana and months before national Prohibition. *Several deaths have occurred in Montana caused by drinking bootleg liquor. One young man, apparently in perfect health before he indulged in a bout with what is commonly known as moonshine, died in agony after a few hours of intense suffering. Two other young men were made violently ill through drinking the same vile decoction, which an alleged bootlegger peddled. The seller has been held to the grand jury by a justice of the peace who conducted an inquiry. It is probable that a man who peddles moonshine or 4 o'clock whiskey has no intention of killing his victim and therefore a charge of murder could not be*

Lincoln County Sheriff Frank Baney with a collection of stills.

maintained. But it seems to us that he could be punished for manslaughter and that should be the fate of any man who, breaking the dry law in the first place, sells or gives to his victims the chemical preparations which cause death or blindness. Probably there are fanatics who will say that the person who patronizes a bootlegger gets what is coming to him, if he is either killed or incapacitated for life, but that is not the humane or popular view of the situation. There are men who will almost sell their souls for a drink of liquor. They are the unfortunate victims of alcoholic disease and are more proper candidates for a hospital than a jail. But avaricious bootleggers should be sent to the penitentiary for a stiff term if they peddle liquor which causes the death of the victim. Nothing but greed is at the bottom of the illicit sales of liquor and no maudlin sentiment should be allowed to stand in the way of conviction of people who sell poison.
[Daily Interlake, Kalispell 8-30-1919]

Less than a year later the next article was written after a score (20) Butte residents died from Moonshine. A doctor explained the many dangers of moonshine and how the number of deaths was much higher than reported.

That "moonshine" whisky is the real cause of many Butte deaths which have been reported as due to other causes is the statement of a well-known Butte physician whose practice covers a wide range. The physician, who stated that he had no wish to pose as an alarmist and had no wish to advertise himself, stated that he is willing to give the facts purely as a matter of civic duty. "That a score of Butte deaths has resulted from bootleg or moonshine whisky," he said, "is, in my opinion, not too large. I base my estimate

on personal experience and on the statements made to me by fellow practitioners... Out of regard for the family, or for other reasons, the cause of death has been camouflaged.

To begin with, Butte, today, is consuming as much liquor as before Prohibition went into effect. Not much beer is drunk, however, this beverage is only found in private homes— a home brew. It follows then, that the present-day tipple is whisky, and more of it is used today than in the palmy days when we had a population of 95,000 and 1917 saloons. Those saloons sold beer chiefly. Today the bootlegger sells moonshine and nothing else.

"Moonshine is derived from three sources, all of them deadly. It is made from wood alcohol, Hoffman's anodyne and from grain alcohol. Wood alcohol corrodes the stomach, causes paralysis of the optic nerves, which results in blindness, causes general paralysis of the nervous system, which produces death. Even in the smallest quantities it is highly injurious to health. Hoffman's anodyne is composed of wood alcohol and ether. This liquid is even worse than wood alcohol in its general effects, if anything could be worse, yet it is a favorite standby of the whisky peddler. Poisonous as arsenic about the grain alcohol moonshine, the harmful ingredient in this is fusil oil. The bootlegger does not know how to extract the fusil oil or else he has not the time nor the equipment to do so.

All grain alcohol 'moonshine' contains fusil oil. Careful investigation, I will wager, will fail to disclose a single bottle of bootleg which does not contain this oil. Now fusil oil has no more place in a beverage than arsenic. Yet it is there and is being consumed daily in large quantities to the *physical deterioration and mental degradation of a large body of the populace." ...*

We have put a ban on the opium and cocaine business, he said, and the colony of dope fiends who once infested Mahoney alley is seen no more. Some of our citizens congratulate themselves and the city on this result. But today, right under our eyes, is going on a traffic that is every bit as deadly, and much more rapid in its effects, than is the traffic in these narcotics.... The health of the public demands that something shall be done to rid us of the curse of the bootlegger. The situation is growing worse instead of better. I do not agree that Prohibition has increased the number of drug addicts. The United States government has that business well in hand. I think I can say, on the contrary, that drug habits are on the decline. The problem that we now must deal with is not the drug peddler, but the bootlegger." This article was originally published in the Butte paper but reprinted in many Montana papers like the Fallon County Times of Baker on June 17, 1920.

Too High A Price

A major risk of drinking moonshine was methanol blindness. Detecting methanol was almost impossible, and consuming more of it would simply get the person more drunk. However, it eventually metabolized into a toxic substance, formic acid. In the body formic acid can have an extremely harmful effect causing permanent optic and partial nerve damage, if not complete blindness. Larger batches of moonshine are more likely to contain methanol. Because methanol is vaporized or evaporated at a lower temperature than alcohol, the first liquid produced by the distillation process usually contains methanol. What follows is a sad story from Kalispell.

Last Saturday a Kalispell high school boy was committed to the state insane asylum, and officials state that the reason is booze furnished him during a recent athletic tournament is directly responsible. There will be those who will censure officials for failure to enforce the law, and others who will hold Prohibition responsible for a condition whereby poison is sold instead of the liquor of pre-Prohibition days, which at worst would have caused nothing more than intoxication. One is the argument of the extreme dry, and the other that of the extreme wet, and so far, as we can see neither of them gets anywhere. We have a Prohibition law, and at the same time we have an illicit liquor industry which it seems impossible to check. The worst thing we can see about present day conditions is the fact that young people are being demoralized by bootleg booze, and our advice to them is to avoid it as they would the plague. The liquor business, except as it applies to physicians' prescriptions, is outside the law and those who engage in it are wholly irresponsible and unscrupulous. The possibility of a jail sentence continually stares them in the face, and they are interested only in something which will insure them quick returns and big profits, regardless of the consequences. They do not hesitate to use industrial alcohol or any other substance to give it a "kick," and often the adulterants they use are fatal. Distilling is also a highly technical process, and the novice may unintentionally produce a brew which will cause blind-

ness, insanity, and even death. All of it is dangerous. In the pre-Prohibition era distillers had a complicated process to remove the poisonous substances, which the moonshiner of today knows nothing of or which he cares less. He is interested only in making his pile before he is caught and unfortunately the youngsters are the best customers, for they do not stop to question the quality. There are always those who will say "the stuff is all right; it came from a responsible man," but it didn't. There is no good liquor, except that which is furnished on prescription, and there isn't enough of that to make even a trickle down the throats of the thirsty in these United States. It may appear to 'be fun to beat the Prohibition law, but blindness or a cell in a mad house is too high a price to pay. Regardless of what one may think of the Prohibition law, there is too much danger in the liquor which is now available to take a chance on it. [Kalispell Inter Lake. March 1928]

Although the article says the boy was sent to the state asylum, he was probably sent to this building to the school for the Deaf and Blind that was located in Boulder, Montana at the time.

Tobacco Valley Moonshine

Research did not reveal any deaths or injuries from moonshine in the Tobacco Valley. This may be attributed to the availability of Canadian safely distilled liquors and the experience of moonshiners in the area. Having given the dangers of moonshine, it must be pointed out that many moonshiners were excellent brewers. Some had been making their products for years. Before Prohibition, distillers had a complicated process to remove the poisonous substances, which the new moonshiner knew nothing about, or he cared less. In the Tobacco Valley the Pinkham area was well known for being a hot bed for the moonshine business.

Madeline Utter in her book Pinkham Pioneers recorded several stories about moonshiners. This first story shows the length that revenue agents would take to find a still and at the same time shows some compassion. Gladyce Stacy Queen Nelson recalled a story about two little sisters, ages five and three. *An older brother was supposed to be babysitting these little girls because Mom and Dad would be gone for a short time. Instead, he decided to go fishing in a little creek that ran nearby. After he had gone, a knock came at the door and the girls answered. There were two gentlemen dressed in suits. They asked if their dad was home. Of course, they said no. Then one of the men stated, "We are revenue men, I hear your dad has a still. Is that right?" The girls said yes. He asked, "Do you know where he keeps it?" And yes, they would show them. So, the two little girls started out and the men followed. The girls got into a lot of underbrush, sat down, and started crying. When the men*

asked them what is wrong, the girls told them "We are lost. We don't know where the still is. We don't know where our house is." The nice men took the girls back to the house then left.

Madeline also tells the story of *a young moonshiner who took a fancy to a girl walking by his house in Eureka on her way to and from high school. He would stop her and talk to her every time he saw her. This went on for six months. At last, he invited her into his house for a cup of tea and she knew that he was a moonshiner. Even so — she saw his good qualities. She said, "I love him." By the end of the school year, they were married. A bit of work was picking up by then and he went into logging. This couple raised a beautiful family. They were real nice people and a credit to the community all through the years... Now this couple has passed on. This goes to say a lot of nice people were moonshiners.*

One man from Pinkham recalled riding with his dad into Eureka where his dad had a regular route. He would pull up to a house and the boy would jump out and leave an order and then they would drive on to the next place and make a delivery.

Moonshine As Medicine

Bill Stacy was caught in the great flu epidemic in 1918 along with most people. Doctor Long prescribed Canadian whisky for a cure-all. Bill guzzled it down! It was prescribed for kids too. It evidently worked as he lived to tell the tale.... Bill remembered making moonshine along with

his dad and others who lived in the Pinkham hills near a cold stream of water. A still he said was built in a variety of ways but the most common was a rock cairn to hold the fire, the boiler set on top with a dome to catch the swim. Cold water was used to condense the steam and run it through copper tubing into a jug or jar. [Utter]

Speakeasies

Prohibition generated a major and permanent shift in American social life. There were only two legal ways to attain whiskey during Prohibition. People could obtain liquor from licensed druggists for "medicinal" purposes or from clergymen for "religious" reasons. Seldom an option! The thirsty turned to speakeasies. What was a speakeasy? Also called blind pig or gin joint, they were places where alcoholic beverages were illegally sold. Speakeasies patrons could legally drink alcohol, they could not legally buy it. They were private, unlicensed barrooms, nicknamed for how quietly you had to speak the "password" to gain entry so as not to be overheard by law enforcement.

Many formerly legal saloons across the country catering only to men closed. In their place businesses set up speakeasies to attract women to get more profits. The competition for patrons in speakeasies created a demand for live entertainment and dances which the already-popular jazz music also inspired. With thousands of underground clubs and the prevalence of jazz bands, liquor-infused partying grew during the "Roaring Twenties." Another new phenomenon began called "dating" when young singles met without parental supervision and another created venue was the house party.

Even though police and custom agents would raid speakeasies and arrest their owners, they were so profitable that they continued to flourish. Speakeasies were generally ill-kept secrets, and owners exploited low-paid police officers with payoffs to look the other way, enjoy a regular drink or tip them off about planned raids by federal Prohibition agents. Bootleggers who supplied these private bars would often add water to good whiskey, gin, and other liquors to sell larger quantities. Some owners resorted to selling still produced moonshine when Canadian produced liquor was hard to find. To hide the taste of poorly distilled whiskey and "bathtub" gin, speakeasies offered to combine alcohol with ginger ale, Coca-Cola, sugar, mint, lemon, fruit juices and other flavorings, promoting the enduring mixed drink, or "cocktail," in the process.

Large cites in Montana had speakeasies, but Butte was the cream of the crop. One Spokane paper said   prohibition never came to Butte. More than 150 speakeasies operated in Butte during Prohibition. Operators could expect their speakeasy to be raided every two to three years during the 13 years of Prohibition. The Spokane Daily Chronicle published a bootlegging exposé by reporter Mark A. Shields about conditions in Butte during Prohibition. He wrote, "Prohibition has not touched Butte. The supply of booze appears to be inexhaustible. Shields and a companion walked into a Butte pool hall and the bartender asked, "What'll you have?" "I chose Scotch," wrote Shields. "Up came the left hand and a pint bottle. My companion called for bourbon and up came the right hand." [Spokane Daily Chronicle 10-24-22]

Because of the number of federal customs and border patrol agents in the Tobacco Valley and its small population there were no speakeasies in the Tobacco Valley. Drinkers had to rely on soft drink establishments and a friendly bartender. Also, an attempt to find a speakeasy location in Kalispell or Whitefish was unsuccessful in either written material or discussions with museum personnel.

How To Be A Successful Bootlegger

Owners of speakeasies often went to great lengths to hide their stashes of liquor to avoid confiscation, but also so that they could not be used as evidence in a trial. The owners built camouflaged doors, had secret wine cellars and false walls. Raids were frequent but since a lot of the proprietors were warned in advance, their places were clean as shot glasses when the police arrived. Early on judges ruled that a search warrant was required to raid one. The editor of the Whitefish Pilot paper ran this tongue-in-cheek editorial early in the years of Prohibition. (May 5, 1921).

"HOW TO BE A SUCCESSFUL BOOTLEGGER" "The Ancient and Parasitic Order of Bootleggers should thrive in Montana. The list of Charter members soon should be a long one. The only qualification for membership is a desire to keep from earning your daily bread `by the sweat of your brow,' plus a desire to violate the law. The first thing is to get an automobile, a 'twin two' will do, as they don't need to be very fast now. The next thing is to go to the border and load your car with 'booze'; then put on the side curtains and start on your way. The officers have no business looking into your car—the Supreme Court says that if the officers 'suspicion' that you have booze in your car, they must take this evidence before the district judge, and he must be convinced that there is reasonable ground for your arrest before a warrant can be issued. While the officers are doing that, of course you can see to it that you are well on your way to some other place and then when the officers 'suspicion' that you have 'booze' they must take the evidence before their district judge, and he must be satisfied before a warrant can be issued. And in the meantime, you can put the 'booze' in your cellar, or your customers can put it in theirs, and when the officers 'suspicion' that it is in the cellar, they must take their evidence before the district judge, and he must again be satisfied that there is cause for action before a warrant can be issued. In the meantime, your customers will have swallowed the evidence. Now you are ready to start on your next trip — and the round of suspicions and trips to the district judge will begin again. Repeat as often as you think necessary. The constitutional rights of booze fighters and bootleggers will be saved."

Rumrunners

The men who smuggled Canadian whisky were rumrunners and they regarded themselves simply as entrepreneurs filling a legitimate demand. They looked down on moonshiners, who supplied a less affluent level of society, were arrested more often and tended to receive stiffer penalties when convicted. While not exclusively so, the actual running of booze across the border was usually conducted by Americans. "Adventurous Canadians occasionally drove loads as far south as Utah or Colorado, but the main problem for the Canadian was finding buyers at his destination without running afoul of local authorities." [Bootlegging and the Borderlands]

Rum Road to Spokane by Edmund Fahey tells his adventures as a rumrunner and his time in jail after being nabbed. His book may be the only one written by a rumrunner. As a young man Fahey in 1923 moved from Montana to take over his deceased stepfather's roadhouse just outside of Spokane, Washington. His memoir, published in 1972, is a fascinating and comprehensive account of his adventures and misadventures in the illegal liquor trade. Upon taking over the tavern, he became dissatisfied with paying rumrunners $70 a case for Scotch whiskey that he could get himself for $36 at a Canadian export house and decided to become his own rumrunner. For two or three days' effort, he could realize a profit of $2,500. As a comparison a dollar in 1920 would be worth 15 dollars today. No wonder so many participated in violating the laws of Prohibition.

Edmund Fahey's book gave us a ton of information on the process of "professional" rumrunning. He found he needn't fear other rumrunners muscling in on him: "The majority of runners were a decent type ... Every man hauled for himself and himself only. There was no organized racket running the smuggling in our area. On several occasions some guy tried to move in and be a big shot, but, in true western fashion, his ambitions were always curtailed. He found, however, that there was no protection from hijackers, who, rather than risking the trip to Canada themselves, would waylay rumrunners, "in the knowledge that any victim who reported his loss would be subject to prosecution by the state."

How A Hijacking Gang Operated

Hijacking was a major problem for rumrunners because they feared going to the authorities to make a complaint. This is how a gang developed in the Havre, Montana area. The hijackers became more and more bold in their operations. At first, they posed as prohibition agents and relieved bootleggers who fell into their clutches of their cargoes of liquor. Then when they found how easy that was, they began to take money, watches and even clothes from some of the rumrunners. Then the hijackers began to take the cars. They had assembled at least 20 automobiles. One rumrunner and possibly two had been killed in a battle with these outlaws when authorities began to realize that they had not only bootleggers to deal with but a well-organized and powerful band of land pirates who preyed upon those engaged in the forbidden traffic. When authorities learned who the leaders were, they fled the state to California. The charge against the men was that of stealing gunny sacks and bottles. In California their attorneys advanced the plea that the theft of gunny sacks and bottles were such a trivial matter as not to warrant the extradition of a man from California to Montana. The courts agreed and the man secured his freedom. [Helena Independent 2-24-22]

A Rumrunner's Death And Hijacking

You would think that rumrunners would often have serious wrecks, but there were surprisingly few reported. *Steve Parsons, alleged to be one of the best known liquor runners in the northwest, was reported to have been killed in an automobile accident near Taft, on the Idaho-Montana line. Parsons' machine was said to have tipped over the grade while traveling at a high rate of speed westward to Spokane with a load of liquor. It is said that two companions were knocked unconscious. While the dead man and the other two were unconscious lying in the ditch, a passerby came upon them, and instead of helping, robbed them of all their liquor and money and drove off. Parsons was arrested last spring for endeavoring to run liquor into Spokane from Northwest Montana. [Billings Gazette 11-8-24] Spokane papers report the arrest came after a 60 to 70 miles per hour chase.*

Even The Streets Of Town Were Unsafe

The Ford car of M. Snyder of the Iowa Flats section was run into and tipped over at the intersection of Dewey Avenue and Sixth Street by a Wyoming car. The Ford had the windshield and top wrecked, but the occupants, Mr. and Mrs. Synder and the children of John Morgan, who were with them, were uninjured outside of the shaking up. [Eureka Journal 7-19-28] In 2013 Gary Montgomery was interviewing ninety year old John Morgan and he mentioned the wreck. "My sister and I were with them (his grandfather and grandmother) we turned to go up the street and a bootlegger was being chased, and he came in behind us and tipped us over. We were just kids." [Montgomery] No doubt there were many such wrecks unreported or unknown.

Everyone Was Bribed

Professional rumrunners were successful only because of bribes. The sums of money being exchanged proved a corrupting influence for federal, state and local level administrators. Police officers and Prohibition agents alike were frequently tempted by bribes or the lucrative opportunity to go into bootlegging themselves.

The Missoulian in 1924 printed the confession of a young rumrunner who had returned to school. He said if he had the money he made in three years he'd be independent for life, but he spent every cent of it being a good fellow and paying for protection, an average of $200 per trip. The most important bribe went to the officer in charge of a certain area. He was the only individual with whom these shady dealings could be transacted. He detailed the men under him and knew their whereabouts at any given time. The regular patrolman never knew what section of the district he would be ordered to cover.

Another bootlegger noted he had been stopped 20 times with a car full of whiskey. He was arrested only once, but his protection money averaged $200 a trip. At every place of importance he left "protection" money. He had the advantage of having with him someone who knew the game and the officials on the route. An inexperienced man probably would have been arrested long before he finished the trip. Tens and twenties were dropped lavishly; he were introduced to many city, county, state and federal officials before many trips had been completed and some of them introduced themselves. When he paid protection money to one man, he had to be careful that another might be envious because he was not in on the rake-off and would "knock him over." When a rumrunner becomes prosperous, his protection rates were raised, and it he complained he was arrested, his cargo and car confiscated. Almost every official had his price, and it had to be paid. Honest dry squad members did work diligently to stop bootlegging.

Fahey further explained the process, "Occasionally, a man who knowingly allowed whisky to move into the States would be transferred to a different district. When that happened, all pay-offs were forgotten until the Canadian Export House could contact another American officer of the law who was willing to take bribes. When a runner started to Canada from the States, he had a fair idea of the conditions existing along the border in the region where he was operating. This was gotten through the grapevine from other runners and friends. This information included which export house offered the best chance for an uninterrupted return trip, physical road conditions, and any changes of Border Patrol personnel.

Advance knowledge was necessary for the successful smuggling of rum. The runner had to be prepared for any emergency. When he left the States for Canada, he never knew whether there was a possibility of a pay-off through the border region. If there was, he would have been told about it at the export house. He would be informed that a certain road would be open at a definite time."

Fahey continued "the runner with proper arrangements knew the Border Patrol's every move and traveled alternate roads to elude it. But obtaining the information needed for all this cost money. You paid your way out when conditions allowed. You made your way in your own way when you had to do so. A knock over now and then of a carload of rum did not keep other cars from making the same run, and they usually got away with it. The efforts of the diligent border officer scarcely showed. He must have realized his job was hopeless, for it wasn't long before he too had his price. For the head man that price was a flat guarantee of $800 per month per runner. That would give him a handsome income with a small clientele.

It must not be taken for granted that the pay-off system existed in every district along the border. In many districts, the honor of the Border Patrol was never dragged through the mire. But whether the district was a pay-off or a closely guarded one, practically the same amount of rum was hauled through it. A greater weakness than corruption was that the Federal Government simply did not furnish the Border Patrol sufficient men or competitive cars."

It was a joke among the Tobacco Valley citizens that if a man got caught bootlegging and had to quit, he could get on as a dry-squadder, and if he got fired as a dry-squadder, he could turn into a bootlegger. Emmett Quirk claimed, "the dry squad left here with more money than what the bootlegger did."

A joke among bootleggers. First Bootlegger "How's business Bill?" Second Bootlegger replies "Fine. Fine, I've got two new judges, and a district attorney, on my payroll and two judges, a chief of police and prohibition agent ready to sign next week."

Smuggling In Canadian Booze

Canadian provinces, realizing that money could be made off alcohol, quickly adapted to accommodate their neighbors south of the border. British Columbia instituted Prohibition in 1917. They quickly realized the potential and voted to do away with their own Prohibition in 1921. Beginning in 1920, the trade from Canada became paramount and provinces enjoyed a highly taxed American trade. Each Canadian province set up its own export houses, which charged a high duty on all liquor destined for the United States. The export houses were not allowed to sell to Canadians who had to buy from provincial liquor stores. The export houses were in towns that had easy access to the United States, with departure points near mountains off the beaten track of the U.S. border patrol. Fernie, British Columbia was just perfect at only 40 miles to the Border.

The hospitality and organization offered by Canadian individuals and export companies undoubtedly facilitated the American liquor smuggler. In the coal-mining town of Fernie, British Columbia one "Mister Big" [his real name was Jack Wilson] operated a two-story brick garage that contained not only liquor storage, but a repair shop and sleeping area for tired customers. Cars usually began pulling in about 3:00 in the afternoon. While the vehicles were loaded and serviced, their drivers spent the afternoon in the pool hall or at a card table playing high-stakes poker with local businessmen. [Bootlegging and the borderlands] In Fernie, a relic of the rum running days still stands. It is the old dairy on 1st Avenue, now Total Attraction Hair Design, which was the export house that supplied the elusive Mr. Big for many years.

Export houses were private enterprises licensed by the government to export alcoholic beverages. According to law they were to haul the booze to some place on the border, then give it to the exporter and watch it leave Canada. Only U.S.-bound liquor was subject to the Canadian export duty which rumrunners gladly paid because that cost would be more than offset by the high profits of sales. From the section above about bribes one can see how these private export houses collaborated with the rumrunners to help them and keep their own business prosperous.

There were groups opposed to Prohibition and they published newspaper ads on why it was not good for the nation or Montana. In "Facts of Prohibition Number Eleven" they pointed out the money Montana lost to their neighbors on her northern border. In 1928 they recorded the tax revenue from the three provinces: British Columbia, $2,752,229; Saskatchewan $600,600; Alberta, $2,761,009 on booze going into Montana. Ten years before in 1918 Montana collected $363,000 in liquor revenues and none after. After pointing out these statistics the ad asks: *Do you prefer that state of affairs to some system such as your northern neighbors have adopted? It is, of course, distinctly your privilege to decide the question. But you cannot do so. The Federal government denies that privilege. That is why the Eighteenth Amendment is a blot on the Constitution. Remember when you vote: The ballot is the cure for the evils of national Prohibition.* [Daily Interlake 10-24-1930] The ad was an attempt to get voters to support anti- Prohibition candidates. Montana, like many states, struggled to replace the lost income from booze taxes.

Rumrunners' Cars

Most rumrunners engaged an experienced helper; Fahey's helper was a one-armed driver-mechanic named Ray, "one of the most able drivers who ever forced a car with a load of booze, and very handy at repairs along the road." Ray knew all the back roads of the border country and was well acquainted with farmers and ferrymen along the route who could be paid and trusted, as well as border officials who could be bribed.

Rumrunning required a big powerful car and the best heavy plied tires you could buy. When modifying a car to make a moonshine runner, subtlety was the first rule. The vehicle had to look "stock" — it could not have any flashy modifications that would make the car attract attention. Three out of four cars on the road were Model T Fords.

Capable of up to 45 mph and priced at $250, the Model T ("Tin Lizzie") was everywhere, making it possible for the bootlegger to blend in. The auto magnate Henry Ford was a staunch teetotaler, but the car that made him rich also became the most popular bootlegging car of the Prohibition Era. Early bootleggers could move ninety gallons of booze in a Model T, which was worth $4,000. Most bootleggers used stock Model Ts, but some added false bottoms to hide the alcohol with cargo like live chickens on top. The Model T was produced for 18 years beginning in October 1908. It was replaced by the Model A in 1927.

Ford Model T

Others common cars confiscated by agents included Chrysler Coupes, Studebakers, Buick Touring cars, and Chevrolet Coupes. While they experimented with different cars over time, the modified cars were never quite fast enough. Then Ford came along and unintentionally created the perfect moonshine delivery vehicle. Mechanics found that they could easily trick-

Ford Model A

out the V-8 engine to get a bit more speed…and this made all the difference in outrunning the law. Some even used the most powerful V-8 they could buy at that time: an ambulance engine.

Engines were "souped-upped" by modifications that included adding more carburetors so the car could burn more fuel, installing new intake manifolds to bring more air to engine, and over boring the cylinders to increase the car's displacement for more horsepower. These cars didn't only need to drive fast, they needed to haul a whole lot of weight. Typically carrying 100 to 180 gallons of moonshine, these vehicles needed to drive at high speeds while carrying almost 800 pounds of alcohol — and they had to do it on twisting, curving backwoods dirt roads. The suspensions of the moonshine runners were so stiff that the rear of the car would be high up in the air when there is no moonshine inside but would appear normal once the car was loaded. On the trip north, most of these cars carried sandbags so that the car did not ride suspiciously high when empty.

To prevent the police from tracking them down, bootleggers would use "borrowed" license plates during their runs. It worked! One clever rumrunner used license plate No. IK-780 from Great Falls in 1929. The investigation of the automobile license showed it was issued to the Great Falls police department. Colonel Charles L. Sheridan, collector of customs, saw the license on a car engaged in rumrunning near Warland, between Libby and Eureka. The rumrunner car was a Packard sedan fitted for booze running, the springs being strengthened, the rear cushions removed, and seat leveled. An attempt was made to find the owner of the car, but without success. The car, Colonel Sheridan said was one on the regular bootlegger trail. [Helena Independent Record 3-4-1929]. Fahey mentioned having five sets of license plates in his car.

They would also install switches that would turn their taillights and brake lights off to help them throw off any revenue agents on their tail. Boiler plating protected the gas tank from bullets.

Less accomplished individual bootleggers would hide booze under false floorboards with felt padding or in fake gas tanks. Sometimes whiskey was literally mixed with the air in the tire tubes. To fool authorities at the border, a smuggler might have a woman and child inside his car with hidden liquor, booze was even found stowed inside a school bus transporting children.

"Virtually all of the rumrunners are known by patrolmen and when one appears in a border town his actions are closely observed and when he disappears the vigilance of the patrolmen is redoubled and is maintained until the runner is caught or his escape is reported." (Knowing and catching were two different things!) Many runners are preceded by a pilot car which, when caught, flashes its lights on and off and the runner, thus warned, turns around and beats it back to Canada with his contraband goods." [Charles L. Sheridan]

Pilot cars were an effective device for rumrunners. When the dry squad stopped a pilot car the following vehicles would stash their booze, hide their car in some gulley, or take another route. The rule about the vehicle had to look "stock" applied only when they were away from the border country. In practice, those truly serious about the rumrunning business made little effort to conceal their loads but relied instead on speed and durability. Fahey mentions how rumrunners and law officials often socialized together near border towns in both Canada and the United States.

Most Rumrunners Escape

This story confirms the fact that women were treated more leniently, and most runners escaped the clutches of the law. *Local enforcement officers have been more fortunate the past ten days than in sometime and as a result three cars and a quantity of booze have been taken. The first catch was near Dickey Lake last week, when Customs Officer Schrupp and Officer Armstrong intercepted a large Hudson touring car with a load. The driver made good his escape in the darkness, but the car and load were brought on to Eureka. Sunday night the force at Gateway was successful in grabbing a car between that place and Rexford. A man and woman were in the car, the man, making good his escape, but the woman was captured. She gave her name as Jane Newton and was released under $25 bond after appearance before U. S. Commissioner Pomeroy. Tuesday night another large car was captured on one of the roads leading from Canada, the driver in this case also abandoning his load in time to make escape.* [Eureka Journal 5-25-27]

Charles L. Sheridan

Charles L. Sheridan, who is quoted many times, was Montana's most famous war hero from World War One. He was awarded the second highest award, the Distinguished Service Cross, which is confined to anyone who may distinguish himself or herself by extraordinary heroism in connection with military operations against an armed enemy of the United States under circumstances which do not justify the award of the Medal of Honor. He was one of only 53 Montana's soldiers in WWI to be awarded the Distinguished Service Award. His citation reads: "Charles L. Sheridan, Captain, Company A, One Hundred and Sixty-Third Infantry. For extraordinary heroism in action on Hill 230, near Cierges, France, July 31 and August 1, 1918. He demonstrated notable courage and leadership by taking command of the remnants of two companies and leading them up the hill and into the woods against violent fire from the enemy. He personally shot and killed three of the enemy and under his direction six machine guns were put out of action and the hill captured." He was wounded three different times during the war.

President Cooledge named Sheridan Montana's Collector of Customs which was a political appointment meaning he could be replaced by the next President. President Hoover continued him in his job. He served for eight years. For most it would be a cushy job, but being a soldier, Sheridan became instantly involved in enforcement of the Volstead Act. He also gave many speeches to service groups and gave newspapers interviews to keep people up to date on the progress of enforcement.

Coal Trains

Automobiles were not the only means of smuggling booze. The coal trains that crossed the border were ideal for smugglers. When Prohibition began most smuggling was done by placing booze in the coal. Coal was used for heating in many places. The Great Northern built a line into the Crows Nest Pass area in Alberta, Canada from their line in the Tobacco Valley. The end of that coal line was Michel, British Columbia, Canada where it was loaded into their rail cars. Smugglers would hide their goods in those railcars heaped high with coal someplace before the border.

Freight trains sometimes had 60 to 70 cars filled with coal and Custom Agent Art Fleming tapped through each car with a long pole. It was nothing to be tapping away and all of a sudden be greeted with the tinkle of breaking glass and have liquor fumes drift up in my face." he said. Fleming's biggest catch was 52 cases of whiskey in a single

A tripple is place where coal cars are loaded or emptied. Tobacco Valley Museum photo

car. Fleming also said that all the bottles of liquor that was confiscated at Gateway in the early years had to be sent to Great Falls. Later they were given the authority to destroy them. [Daily Interlake 8-13-57]

At the time all trains were powered by steam engines pulling a tender. A tender is a special rail car containing the coal and water. The Great Northern had tender loading chutes at Rexford, Whitefish, and Libby. Leo Collar's father told him he often saw or heard bottles breaking as the coal slid down the chutes.

The problem for rumrunners was they had to mark the car to keep track of the car with their booze or it would be lost or hijacked. The second big problem was that all members of the train crew had to be paid off as well as others along the way. Everyone was paid off from the sellers, loaders, unloaders, train agents, spies etc. To prevent hijacking of

Great Northern Box Coal Loader at Michel, British Columbia. Michel is a ghost town today. Tobacco Valley Museum photo

their booze rumrunners had to always keep track of the car at stops. After being loaded they kept an eye on their coal car until it began its journey south, then at every stop, and at Rexford or Whitefish where the smuggled liquor would generally be removed from the railcar when safe to do so. Farley devoted a chapter of his book to how he smuggled liquor in a coal train. There are many articles about finding booze in coal cars, sometimes by workers unloading the coal, it was a frequent method of smuggling for both the amateur or more professional rumrunner.

Bill Hoover, J.E. Brice, Art Fleming in Gateway Custom House Garden 1914. Tobacco Valley Museum photo

Other Choices for Smuggling Across the Border

Sometimes when it was too hot with agents, rumrunners hired a pack train from a friendly Canadian ranch to haul booze over heavily timbered mountain trails to a predetermined location on the American side, where it would be picked up. A good packer could strap in five cases per animal. A border patrolman from Eureka, Frank "Boots" Combs, patrolled on horseback areas not accessible by auto along the border from the Continental Divide to the Cascades in Washington as part of his official duties. He was a customs agent for 47 years. There was no mention of a pack train ever being intercepted in Northwest Montana, but Col. Charles Sheridan mentioned them as one problem for customs inspectors.

Sheridan also mentions that during the winter bobsleds were hired and the open geography of the Tobacco Plains made easy traveling for dog teams. Another method of rumrunning was the use of rafts to float down the Kootenai River with their moonshine. Irene Abby recalled a man asked her carpenter dad to build flatboats to use in June when the water was high and easy to float. He would load them at the border and then near Rexford a car or truck would be waiting to pick up the load of liquor to deliver it to the destination. He lost most of his first load when he hit the rapids, struck a rock, and overturned. He lost 5000 dollars! No problem! Three days later his second load made it. He made a lot of money rumrunning, but unfortunately, he was drunk one day and was killed at the railroad crossing in Rexford.

J.A.B. MacDonald (Customs Officer at Newgate 1911-1939) was a religious person, very conscientious in discharging his duties. Smuggling of any kind concerned him very much. He spent many nights on the riverbank watching for rumrunners on the river, often with success. [Shea] One time agents caught smugglers in board daylight.

A couple of whiskey smugglers, grown over-bold by frequent whiskey successes floated down the Kootenai river in a boat loaded with some 50 cases of whiskey. Evidence they had grown over-bold lay in fact that both had so frequently sampled their cargo that its influence was being felt.

They were having a very good time when their craft floated across the internation line at Gateway instead of waiting for dark. It just happened such was their luck that two federal officers were near the river on a little Sunday morning hunt trip. The were, after venison, but when the boat with its happy crew drifted into sight all thoughts of lesser game vanished. They took the booze and gave the owners their liberty. [Western News 10-29-20]

Once in 1922 booze was brought into Eureka instead. Seven trunks were unloaded at the Eureka depot. No one claimed the trunks; inside were 299 bottles of fine liquor. A few months later a judge ordered Sherriff Baney to destroy the booze. Baney learned not to destroy bottles in the dump as was a common practice; pouring bottles into the Kootenai River worked better.

One simple method of rumrunning was shown by the author's great uncle when "Sam McCarty was arrested for carrying a sack of booze on his back." (Eureka Journal 1-19-28) Sam had a hard time making a living after Prohibition started. He had a bar in Rexford and no doubt was trying to supply his customers with the good stuff.

Booze Smugglers Take To The Air

Less than two years into Prohibition rumrunners found a new way to cross the border. With arrest, or even death, staring them in the face with every trip into the states, some ingenious smugglers turned to safer and more sane methods where they would not be annoyed by the fear of being arrested. Accordingly, they reasoned their salvation was to take to the air. Of course, they had government help! An acknowledged mechanic could acquire a Curtiss Jenny biplane after World War One. The military disposed of those surplus planes by disassembling, then crating and shipping them, complete with instructions for reassembly.

For weeks, even months, reports have been drifting down from Northern Montana that lonely farmers have heard during the early morning hours what appeared to them to be the whirring of an airplane propeller. Rushing to their darkened doorways, their only reward was to hear the purring sound disappearing in the distance. With these reports persistently reaching their ears, the officers are endeavoring to conceive some way to cope with the new situation that has arisen. To them, stopping automobile rumrunners is only a matter of course. They are also familiar with the usual methods of smuggling booze across the international line, but as yet they have to conceive some method of constructing a Jacob's stepladder whereby, they can hope to come in direct contact with the modern bootlegger who loads his cargo into his airplane and goes soaring high above the heads of the craning necks of the officers and their old enemies, the hijackers. [Choteau Montanian 8-10-

1922]

There were several instances in Montana where a plane crashed with booze. Sometimes rumrunners didn't own the planes, they stole them. It wasn't until 1926 that Customs asked for two aircraft to patrol the Montana skies.

Loading a biplane

Why Own When You Can Steal

Not just airplanes were stolen, but cars. Rumrunners who ply between Butte and the Canadian border were common auto thieves in Butte. The whisky runner had the hazard of losing his own car if he was intercepted on a trip and there lies the reason for numerous auto thefts. In most cases stolen cars were returned to the city by officials when rumrunners abandoned the cars or agents arrested them. Upon returning, successful runners left their stolen cars in places where officers could readily locate them. The Butte police chief stated that speedometers on stolen cars that have been recovered several days after they disappeared would often show that it had been driven 500 miles, which would indicate a trip to Canada and back. [Billings Gazette 3-10-1926]

The Information Pipeline

Fahey wrote, "It is amazing how occurrences on rum road became so quickly and accurately the topic of conversation among the people living along the route in the border territory. Prospectors, woodcutters, and out of the way farmers could tell rumrunners about events that they (the rumrunners) themselves had taken part in on your last trip into the region." The escapades of the rumrunners made exciting gossip that broke the monotony of their everyday lives. It was also this network that often told them when it was safe to cross the border.

Sometimes the runners will wait for a week or two weeks at border points waiting for the customs men to be called away so that they may cross the line. "At Rooseville,' continued Colonel Sheridan, "during the winter as many as 10 and 15 cars were parked at Brown's and Bedner's waiting to cross the border.

Roosville is just across the border in Canada and Brown and Bedner are Canadian bonded truckmen who haul liquor from Fernie, B. C, to the line. They also maintain a garage at Roosville where many of the rumrunners receive accommodations.

Roosville and Gateway

There is some confusion concerning Roosville and Gateway. First, while Sheridan called the border crossing "Rooseville" it was really Roosville named after the Roo family. Roosville was a land crossing five miles east of the Kootenai River. In 1898 Roosville became the first border station established in Montana. Just a few years later, in 1901, the Great Northern Railway, needing coal for its engines, decided to run a spur line from Jennings, Montana north to Fernie, B.C. The most practical route was on the east bank of the Kootenai River. Where the rails crossed into Canada became the natural site for locating the construction headquarters, with the hotels, saloons, eating places and general stores to supply the needs of these rough, but well-paying customers. A few months ahead of the tracks Canadian customs office moved to the new town called Gateway on the United States side and Newgate on the British Columbia side of the border. Without the border they would have been one town.

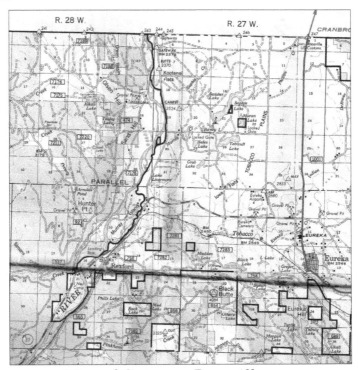

Map of Gateway-Roosville area

Gateway offered a smuggler a choice: the river, the road, or the railroad. Flags are at the border.

American customs followed the Canadian customs into Gateway. After railroad construction ended, Gateway slowly declined as a town, but customs continued as passenger and freight trains as well as road traffic continued to warrant local custom agents. The status of Roosville was unclear but appears basically to be unused. With Prohibition Gateway again bloomed. There were several law-enforcement officers whose duties took them into Gateway, and some lived there with their families. Liquor smuggling was occurring on the river, on the trains, and by auto at Gateway. A station was established as an "Area Headquarters" in Gateway, Montana in July 1924 to help with liquor smuggling. The Whitefish Border Patrol Station, the technical name for the border sector, stationed agents at Gateway, Rexford, and Eureka.

Most of the smuggling occurred around Gateway in the first years of Prohibition. *The Gateway country is said to be infested with rum runners who find it an easy place to slip across the border with their illicit cargo. The country is wild and hilly, covered with forest, groves of small trees and brush. There have been a number of exciting incidents along that section of the border since Canadian whisky is reported to have become so widely demanded south of the line.* [from a report in 1922]. A common practice of smugglers when encountering a border control point was to simply drive a couple of miles and create an unauthorized crossing point. It was no different in the Tobacco Valley. As a result, the five miles between Gateway and Roosville allowed rumrunners to cut the boundary fence, quickly cross

Bird's-eye view of the Gateway area.
Tobacco Valley Museum photo

the border, and then drift back onto the road someplace between the border and Eureka or Rexford.

With more and more autos in the country and roads improved, action around Roosville increased. By 1927, Roosville was once again very active and had almost double the auto traffic. Enforcement activities increased at Roosville.

When the Great Northern ceased services on the route in 1935, the customs station at Gateway closed. The Gateway location is now underwater because of the construction of the Libby Dam and the creation of the Lake Koocanusa Reservoir in 1974. There is a small community on the west side of Lake Koocanusa in Canada still named Newgate and a small settlement north of the border called Roosville.

Art Fleming customs agent at Gateway.

Rumrunning Began Slow

When Prohibition began in Montana in 1919 there was no road to Libby from Eureka and a very poor road to the Flathead Valley. The first car over the road to Whitefish happened in June 1911, but for years the road was basically unpassable. [Eureka Journal 6-9-11] The result of there being few cars and road conditions, most smuggling was done on the railroad through Gateway and mostly buried in coal cars. Change was coming!

The Theodore Roosevelt International Highway was planned as a transcontinental highway through the United States from Portland, Maine, to Portland, Oregon, with a total length of about 4,060 miles. The highway was designated a memorial after Roosevelt's death and followed much of Highway 2, but the designated route in Northwest Montana went north to Eureka and then south to Libby where it hooked back onto Highway 2. After World War One there was a push to improve roads and money flowed into Northwest Montana to work on the TR Highway. With Lincoln and Flathead Counties also funding the work, the road from the Flathead Valley to the Tobacco Valey was considered a good road by 1921. There was still no road to Libby, but work was ongoing and finally in July 1924 the new road to Libby was opened and ready for rumrunners. During the first two years of Prohibition, few autos crossing the border at Gateway were found to have booze.

Get Set Go

Imagine the excitement when those waiting rumrunners learned the coast was clear. The few customs agents remaining reacted. It was a pastime of local Tobacco Valley teenagers to watch the chases between the law and bootleggers. Sometimes to hide the evidence, rumrunners would throw the booze out in the roadside brush as they sped away from the law. The kids would retrieve the unbroken bottles and sell, trade, or try it themselves. [Frederickson] Adults would often sit on the drumlins at night watching the lights of the rumrunners below as they drove wildly across the plains often with a law officer in pursuit.

Everyone seemed to know the nights when the action was going to take place. The rumrunners had their own net-

This garage was a stop for many rumrunners. TR stood for Teddy Roosevelt Highway now known as Highway 37. Tobacco Valley Board of History photo.

work. They knew where they could find a mechanic if they needed it, where to buy gasoline (most carried their own to not have to), and where to lay low if needed. Some ranchers living close to the border made available, for a modest commission, their barns or haystacks, which rumrunners used to conceal caches of liquor. The illicit product could then be smuggled to its destination at the runner's convenience. Emmet Quirk recalled finding a smuggler's booze in one of their barns and Shea recalled finding a smuggler's car in a ravine. John Stoken recalled the story of a rumrunner who turned up Grave Creek, crossed a bridge and pulled into Matt Stoken's. Matt had two piles of hay and 50 cases of liquor were stashed in the hay. It was a month before the man returned for his liquor. Matt worried the whole time the revenue agents might show up. The moonshiner gave him a case for his trouble.

Mike Marvel recalls the story of his grandfather's big barn in Rexford. Fred Marvel had worked in the coal mines at Fernie, and no doubt had connections. He had draft horses and a fake storage area underneath their stalls in the barn. Rumrunners could stash their booze under the planks when they needed a place to hide their liquor and maybe some of it was Fred's. Once the booze reached Eureka it could be sent anywhere. For example, the undertaker for Libby and Eureka received many bottles of embalming fluid that had to be returned. They were sent back filled with moonshine. [Gruber]

Warland, between Rexford and Libby, was in the middle of nowhere during Prohibition and Earl Hansberry's father built a garage in 1924 when the road was built connecting

Rexford with Libby. The T R Garage was a rumrunners paradise. In an interview Earl and his wife, Helen, describes the scene. "The country was dry then. These booze runners from Canada come down, they all filled their gas up and they all stopped there 'cause it was out of the way." Helen added: "He (Earl's dad) was bad as they were. He run 'em into his garage, fix their cars. Us girls would go down there, and they had all the windows covered over. Not a bit of light showed for the guys comin' along lookin though them. Ma used to get so mad at us 'cause we'd go down there." Earl: "They said they'd come across the line up there (at Gateway) and they'd hold 'ern, maybe sometimes for a week, 'til the Federal guys weren't around and they'd give 'ern the go ahead and maybe 25, 30 of them cars come across the line at once." Helen: "We went to a dance at Rexford one night and comin' back early in the morning we were stopped by the (Federal) guy looking for whiskey. They stopped us, stuck their old shotguns through the door of the car and wanted to know who we were."

Women Bootleggers

Women bootleggers (moonshine smugglers) were not unheard of; in fact, there may have been more women bootleggers than men. Here's why: women had substantial advantages over men. The court system and politicians just didn't have the stomach for putting mothers and grandmothers behind bars. Most women were earning money just to keep a roof over their family's head and food on the table. Another advantage for women over men: it was illegal to search a woman in many states in those days. Women took full advantage of this and actually hid moonshine on their persons; some even taunted law enforcement to search them. Art Fleming for 29 years a custom officer, most at Gateway and Roosville, noted that the funniest incident he had was a "proper looking woman sitting on a bottle of liquor."

Dan Dooley on horseback. Glacier National Park photo

Colonel Sheridan noted that women conceal smuggled goods in their clothing and since there is no woman inspector in Montana, they are not apprehended until the inspector was positive that they were smuggling something more dangerous than booze. When an agent was certain of her

Josephine Dooley was more than a moonshiner. Glacier National Park photo

conviction, he requested that a woman inspector be sent out from St. Paul and the woman was apprehended and searched on her next trip.

When making moonshine, women kept a low profile and were not confrontational; if a woman was caught, she did not have a hard time convincing the sheriff that the discovered still wasn't hers. Theresa Otto in an article for "Distinctly Montana" covers the stories of many Montana women bootleggers including John Fraley's story of the most famous of all, Josephine Dooley from Glacier Park.

Blow The Whistle For A Quart

Josephine Dooley purportedly killed a man in Colorado, ran to Montana and became a dance hall girl in McCarthyville. McCarthyville was a railroad boom town on the Great Northern Railway line at Marias Pass. The town attracted the usual lowlifes who follow railroad builders. The hospital's doctor was so bad "you never knew how many men had died until the spring thaw." When Josephine got addicted to opium, she was kidnapped and brought to his remote property by a love-struck Dan Dooley to dry out. Dan Dooley was a prospector, outfitter, and one of Glacier National Park's first rangers.

The Great Northern built a siding by Josephine's and Dan's ranch so Jim and Louis Hill's private car could stop. The Hill family loved the little woman with her great cooking, rough language, and big earrings. Meanwhile, Dan was one of the first park rangers who did a little trapping and poaching within the confines of the park he was being paid to police. He was later fired for 'excessive' poaching of the park's wildlife. His loss of income was no doubt made up by his wife. Josephine operated several stills on that ranch and her product was so well-known that passing train engineers would stop and blow their whistles to signal the number of quarts they wanted delivered.

A Hot Water Bottle Works Great

A couple of months into Montana's Prohibition bootleggers, rumrunners and moonshiners were testing the waters so to speak. Women in Butte came up with ingenious ways to serve liquor. *How women bootleggers operate in Butte is related by a Helena man who visited the copper metropolis. He calls them "bustlesqueezers". According to this authority, who denies that he bought a drink, but knows a friend who did, the peddlers of booze are invariably well dressed women, who have a roving eye and a friendly disposition. Upon sighting a prospective customer, the lady engages him in conversation and learns during their talk that he would buy for as swell a looker as she, if he had the chance, the*

lady smiles sweetly and says maybe she can afford the opportunity. Seeking a secluded spot, she produces a glass from a handbag and presents it to the customer. Then she takes a tube from her corsage, and leaning against a convenient wall, a fairly good quality of booze flows from the tube into the glass. "Fifty cents, please," says the charmer and as the astonished customer forks over the money she explains hurriedly how the scheme works. "I have a hot water bag filled with liquor," she says. "To this a tube is attached. You noticed me leaning back against the wall? Well, the pressure forces the booze up through the tube and there you are." [Eureka Journal 4-3-1919] Soon after there was no need for water bottles as booze was served openly in Butte.

Whispering Willy Watkins Salesmen And Bootlegger

Not just women dressed in flowing oversized clothing. Mr. William Payne became the first Watkins salesperson in the Tobacco Valley area to deliver goods to a customer's door. He had black pepper and red pepper, vanilla and other extracts, dry mustard and sage for homemade sausage or chicken dressing to please all the good cooks. He had red liniment or white liniment for aches and pains, menthol camphor salve for colds and coughs, Old Red Barn salve for scrapes and bruises. Mr. Payne became a pain killer by selling products to alleviate pain.

Bill was a good salesman. He had rather unique qualities that helped. His voice came out in a whisper. He was soon known to his neighbors as "Whispering Willy." When he related the news of the community at his stops it sounded as if he was sharing their secrets. Willy was often asked to share a family meal. He gladly accepted. They could hear more about their neighbors, and he wouldn't have to go home and eat alone. Children got to know him. When they heard his Model-T come they shouted, "Ma, here comes Whispering Willy!"

Bill was a fair man to deal with. If a homesteader didn't have the money to pay, which most didn't, he would make a trade. He took jars of home-canned jelly or jam, milk, butter, eggs, a hunk of venison or vegetables from the garden. He even traded for jugs of moonshine. Prohibition started him into another business. Since he sold Watkins products over the Tobacco Valley area and into Canada, it was easy for him to become a Whiskey Runner. He couldn't compete with the big wheels, but it was a lucrative business on the side. Whispering Willy wore a long black overcoat as his habitual attire. As he was short and his back was bent, sometimes the overcoat would drag in the snow. The coat had huge pockets where he could stash bottles of booze. Willy was very willing to reach deep down into a pocket to exchange moonshine for greenbacks when approached by certain people. [Utter]

Whispering Willie Arrested

W. H. Payne of Rexford and Joe Avery and George Micho of Warland, were given preliminary hearings Monday afternoon in Justice of the Peace court on a bootlegging charge.

They waived examination and were bound over to the district court. These men were apprehended Saturday by Sheriff Baney somewhat out of the usual manner. Sheriff and Mrs. Baney had been at Eureka and were returning home when they met Payne crossing the bridge at Rexford. Payne was carrying a packsack, which by its contour, looked suspicious and Sheriff Baney stopped him and asked him what he had in the sack. He replied that it was grape juice, but Sheriff Baney asked to see and upon examining the sack found jugs containing two and a half gallons of moonshine. Payne was put under arrest and brought to Libby.

Avery and Micho were picked up near Warland on the same trip. These two men were driving a Ford car which had stalled and which they were attempting to repair. The car was in such a position that Baney could not get by, and as he stopped his car, he noticed a quantity of liquor in the Ford. Investigation disclosed 24 bottles of Canadian beer and seven quarts of U. S. whiskey. The Ford car, with Avery and Micho, was brought to Libby, Mrs. Baney driving in their car with one prisoner and Sheriff Baney following with the two others.

In district court Monday Avery pleaded guilty to liquor in possession and as it was his first offense he was let off with the minimum, a fine of $200 and sixty days in the county jail. His partner, Micho, was exonerated as Avery assumed all the blame and stated that Micho was just a passenger in the car. In the case of Payne, a sentence like Avery's was imposed, but it is probable that on account of his poor health a pardon may be secured [Eureka Journal 9-23-26]

Overnight Felons

John and Jane Doe were two of the most popular offenders of those arrested. Many hid their identity behind these pseudonyms. In dealing with repeated offenders investigators discovered that among the defendants whose cases were pending very many second, third and even ninth-time offenders, [Eureka journal 6-28-23] For a rumrunner it might have paid not to carry identification.

Regardless of rumrunner or moonshiner, Prohibition created a host of "overnight felons" involved in various levels in the liquor trade. In the Northwestern United States, Prohibition spawned a group of lawbreakers most of whom, unlike the gangster bootleggers in large cities farther east, had never before engaged in criminal activity.

Who were these new felons? Court records are full violators and their fines. Western News Paper mentioned that Montana was full of Bootleggers and maybe only one in ten was caught. There were so many bootlegging arrest that in 1923 Sheriff Kelley of Lake County was forced to move his office from the county jail to make room for an army of bootleggers awaiting trial. Although a few spent time in prison, by the time Prohibition was repealed, most had returned to a law-abiding life.

Dry Squads

Dry Squad was a term the public used for agents who tried to enforce the Prohibition law regardless of if they were local, state, or federal border patrol or federal custom agents. Mostly dry Squad members were young men, a few in other states were women. Both federal and local governments struggled to impose their laws. Federal enforcement was initially assigned to the Internal Revenue Service and later transferred to the Justice Department and the Bureau of Prohibition. Raids by the "Dry Squad" made for sensational headlines in the newspapers from that period. But how effective they were is debatable. Prohibition agents

A Dry Squad in Washington state. Federal, state, county and local law enforcement authorities were responsible for enforcing Prohibition. This 1919 photo is from the Library of Congress Courtesy of University of Washington.

and cooperative local law enforcers throughout the country seized warehouses full of whiskey, busted up stills, smashed countless bottles of liquor, took axes to beer barrels, and dumped the contents into gutters and sewers. When local Lincoln County officials arrested violators, they were tried at Libby, those who federal agents arrested were tried in Great Falls. Often both federal and local agents participated in an operation.

Col. Charles L. Sheridan: "Many of the inhabitants of the border towns are in league with the rumrunners and keep them informed by telephone or flashlight signals as to the whereabouts of the customs men." Before he died, John Ellis related this story to the author. His mother, Barbara Vukonich Ellis was dating a man who liked to take her on drives out to the border. On some days he insisted she wear a large blooming hat and other days she was told to wear a different hat. She never gave it a thought until years later when he told her the large hat was a signal for rumrunners that the coast was clear. When the dry squads were near, she didn't wear the hat. Her hat could easily be seen from the Canadian side of the border.

Another View Of Montana Enforcement

In 1924 problems of Enforcement in Montana were stated by Montana's federal director of Enforcement. *The people of the country vote dry, and drink wet in the opinion of Addison K. Lusk. He stated that law enforcement depends on the attitude of the people and most people do not back the law. However much has ' been accomplished in Mon-*

tana and as far as crime, poverty, and disease attributable to liquor is concerned, there has been a marked improvement…. The problem in Montana is particularly hard. The state has the longest Canadian border of any in the union… At Fernie, 100 miles north of Kalispell, an export house is operated, and the orders of American bootleggers are filled there, delivered at the border and smuggled over at night… No state is like Montana. This state has more moonshine than any state in the union except in the south. Bonded and cut liquor is sold. The cut liquor is bonded liquor which has been opened and the bottles partly filled with moonshine. In a recent raid at Billings were seized a complete outfit of bonded liquor labels, seals, branded corps, etc., which is used to put up so-called bonded liquor…. The Flathead Courier (Polson, Mont.), January 03, 1924. Today Addison Lusk would be considered head of the Border Patrol and

Just across the border was the Roosville Hotel. "During prohibition people from the states would come up to drink and dance," remembers Mary Roo. The customs office down there helped, as long as the people behaved themselves. They all had to come up at the same time. When the dance was over, the customs officer would say, "All aboard for Roosville Port." They'd go and open the gate and they'd all go back. Photo from Gary Montgomery

Charles Sheridan the head of customs. Dry Squads under the Border Patrol worked throughout Montana and Customs agents usually worked closer to the border.

Authorities Work Together

Canadian whiskey worth almost $3,000 at current prices was discovered buried in a car of Fernie coal here (Spokane) yesterday by deputy sheriffs after Sheriff Long had been notified by Rexford, Mont., officials that they suspected that the car contained liquor. The car from Fernie, consigned to the Great Western Fuel Company, arrived early yesterday morning and was watched carefully for hours until the sheriff learned that the bootleggers had learned that the officers were on guard. It is not known who was to receive the liquor.

When Deputy Sheriffs Bradley, Browne and Wood dug into the coal they found 23 sacks, each containing two dozen pints of Canadian whiskey. While the officers were unloading it, a man shouted to the Deputy Sheriffs that "they had better hurry, the sheriff was watching it. The officials at Rexford observed that the car was being watched there and they notified the sheriff. A fire had been built on the coal in the car by someone who apparently wished to keep warm. One sack of the liquor had been stolen," said Sheriff Long. There were 24 cases to start with, but one sack was empty. This may have resulted in the row which caused the Rexford officials to get suspicious." The liquor is held at the county jail. [Spokesman-Review printed in the Eureka journal 1-12-22]

The Honest Bootlegger

Added to the problem for law enforcement in the early years of Prohibition was "The honest bootlegger" which may seem a paradoxical term, but that is just what Attorney General S. C. Ford is forced to apply to many of the suspects arrested in this state for illicit traffic in liquor. "Many bootleggers", says Mr. Ford, "gravely inform prospective customers that they are not selling them liquor. They speak truthfully. For they are not. Most of the stuff seized, when analyzed, is found to contain anything but liquor: Tobacco juice, red pepper sauce, anything with a 'kick' is peddled.

Of course, under the circumstances, prosecution falls flat. No law is violated, unless the victim wishes to prosecute for false pretense, which as a rule, he does not." [Eureka Journal 6-19-19]

A coal train is crossing the trestle in West Fernie on its way to Rexford. This photo taken in 1912, predates Prohibition. A car was marked so smugglers could retrieve their booze usually in Rexford. Photo from Gary Montgomery

Here Piggy, Piggy: It's Not Always Booze

Federal officers, detailed on prohibition work, have been working in this section and last week made an official visit to Eureka. In stopping the car of Roy Rhodes, they thought they had made a haul when they discovered a suspicious sack lying in the bottom of the car. Taking hold of it the officer was greeted with the vociferous squealing of a young pig, which surprised him so that he hastily dropped it and beat a retreat without further ado. [Eureka Journal 9-9-1920]

It Takes One To Know One

How raids were conducted is shown by this article with the headline: *You Can't Trust a Double Crossing Stool Pigeon.*

Like a thunderbolt out of a clear sky, a "dry" squad of 13 men arrived about 9 o'clock Friday morning and raided the soft drink establishments of this city and several residences and other buildings in which it is alleged liquor is being illegally kept. Six of the places yielded intoxicating liquor, it is reported. Evidence on which the arrests and raids were made was furnished by a "stool pigeon" who went by the name of McFredericks and by another party whose name was not given. Both are said to have been here for several months. McFredericks, an ex-service man, is an affable sort of fellow and worked himself into the good graces of the young people of the community. McFredericks is a sort of bibulous (given to convivial drinking) entertainer himself and participated in some events on which no action is taken by the "dry squad." It is also reported that he is a "dou-

ble-crosser" in another manner which had no connection with his work, and if the report is true his actions in that respect were not only uncalled for but are most disgusting and revolting. Chas Smith, notorious a year or so ago as an alleged bootlegger, is the driver of one of the cars. The whole affair recalls the old sayings in regard to "honor among thieves" and "it takes a thief to catch a thief," and consequently these cases will be watched with interest. [Eureka Journal 8-3-1922]

The next week's headline:

Making Inroads

August 10 — Evidence by which H. P. Shelley, federal Prohibition director for Montana, hopes the bottle neck through which liquor is said to have flowed freely from Canada into Montana by way of Eureka is obtained by a federal agent who "went through the mill." That is, he worked in the lumber mill and when time came for him to gather additional information he dropped a rock on his hand, gave up his job at the mill, obtaining one digging a cellar where he suspected illicit liquor is to be stored. The agent "got in" with the gang to the extent where he on one occasion helped a bootlegger hide liquor when a Prohibition agent arrived in town. In the raid on July 28 on every pool hall, soft drink establishment and hotel, 20 persons were arrested, and much Canadian and Scotch whiskey and even more Canadian beer was seized.

As with most arrests by federal agents, they were bound

over to a federal court in Great Falls. A careful search of the Eureka papers for the next few months found no more information about who was arrested and what they were guilty of. There was a piece of information in the Billings Gazette that mentioned that the arrested violators posted bonds totaling 15,000 dollars.

"It appears that it is not the policy of such officials to furnish the press the names of those arrested." [Western News 8-4-1922] When called, the Federal District Court in Great Falls, Montana related that there is no way to access information from Prohibition cases today.

Northwest Montana Treated Unfairly By Raids

Not just Eureka, but almost, if not all, towns in the Northwest part of the state were victims of raiding Prohibition officers. How unfair the raids could be is evidenced by a raid in Whitefish.

Armed with mimeographed search warrants and affidavits signed by some unknown stoolpigeon supposedly named Ross, a regiment of federal dry agents, divided into squads and made a series of dry raids in and around Whitefish. About a dozen places were searched and quite a contingent of alleged offenders were taken into the local police court and after being given the third degree were handed out hasty and indiscriminate justice in the "give everybody the limit" court presided over by Police-magistrate Ross Van Waggenen.

Local officers knew nothing of the contemplated raid

and the dry army established headquarters out in the timber about three miles from the city, and then telephoned Chief of Police Russell to come out. The chief went well prepared with artillery, assuming that a caravan of professional rum-runners were about to be apprehended, and a valuable cargo taken.

However, what turned out to be raids that netted a few quarts' of "moon" and a considerable quantity of home brew and a few near empty bottles was the result of the carefully planned invasion. While the federal men made the various searches local officers were requested to stand guard.

Places searched were the Glacier Pool Hall, the Glacier Park Cafe, the Elgin Pool Hall, Sharkey Pool Hall, Pastime Pool Hall, Otto White residence, Heine Bassett residence, Payne residence, Vial residence, McArthur's apartments, and Tarr Barber Shop.

The Glacier Park Pool Hall that was conducted by W. W. Arthurs until about 10 days ago when the city closed it, was unlocked by Arthurs to prevent the raiders from breaking in the door. On the premises were found some near empty bottles that are alleged to have been moonshine containers. Arthur's was fined $300. John Rude was taken on a charge of having stills in his possession and was given a fine of $300. Mrs. Rose MacArthur was given a fine of $300, as it was alleged that 'she was in possession of about two quarts of moonshine. Nothing that was considered of real importance was found at the Glacier Park Cafe and no one was brought into court from there. At the Elgin Pool Hall, operated by W. N. Parent, no signs of anything was found, and Parent accompanied the searchers and assisted them in the search.

At the Pastime Pool Hall the searchers found a near-empty bottle that had been thrown by someone, sometime in a wastebasket. Judge Van Waggenen says the bottle had about a teaspoon of what looked like moon in it. Harold Avery, employed at the Pastime was then taken to court as a representative of the establishment was given a fine of $300, which was later reduced to $200. At the Otto White residence no one was at home and the raiders kicked in the door and rummaged through the place but found nothing. Nothing was found at the Sharkley Pool Hall or the Tarr Barber Shop.

The Bassett and Vail residences are said to have revealed a small quantity of moonshine and some home-made brew, the later at the Vail place, and fines were administered. Nothing was found at the Payne residence. Leslie Phoenix who rooms in the rear of the Parent Real Estate office had some home-made wine and he was taken into court and given a fine of $300. All of the search warrants used were based upon an alleged affidavit signed by A.K. Ross, who swore that at all of the various places mentioned he had on some specified date purchased two drinks of moonshine whiskey at 25 cents per drink. The methods of the raiders and the conduct of the local court officers seem to meet general disapproval in several cases, even from those who desire an enforcement of the liquor laws. [Whitefish Pilot 5-31-1927]

In the matter of enforcement of the prohibition in Montana, there are many incidents that appear strange to the average citizen who is on side lines. The Kalispell Monitor paper complained that many people were at a loss to explain why Kalispell and other rural towns were subjected to many raids by the federal enforcement officers while other cities like Butte, Helena, and Great Falls were notorious for their "blind pigs" with liquor was sold openly. The paper noted that in the business district of Kalispell it was doubtful if there was enough liquor sold for even one man to make a living. The paper asked why Kalispell is singled out for many raids in preference to those cities where flagrant violations are going on every hour of the day and night. Kalispell was freer from liquor violations than any other city in Montana. There are no open bars or "blinds" in the business district of Kalispell, and it is very doubtful if there is enough liquor disposed for one man to make a bare living out of that business. [The Flathead Monitor, 1-29-1931]

Rumrunning, Saloon Owner And Criminal

Beryl Holgren in *Looking Back Laughing* wrote about her father's Prohibition years. More common than a raid like that featured above was the undercover agent method. Like all saloons, Harrison Scouten's Eureka establishment, Harry's Place, became a soft drink parlor. With all the dry agents around a bartender had to be careful who he served liquor to.

Papa, always willing to make an extra buck, saw the prospects in bootlegging and entered the business. I have no idea how he slipped across the Line under the noses of the Customs officials, the back seat of his Buick filled with cases of liquor -- fine Scotch whiskeys. I do recall that he gave the Dry Squad a chase one night but managed to elude them. Of course, he may have had a thing going with the Cus-

toms agents who gave him the nod, I guess. He boldly made trips to Butte by train traveling from Eureka to Spokane and from there south on the Milwaukee, a valise packed with hard liquor which he sold to the ACM's (Anaconda Copper Mining Company) VIPs for a handsome sum, ... He made money faster than the Denver Mint. His bootlegging has never troubled me. Almost everyone who dared got into it, respectable businessmen, the less scrupulous, and those in between. And the Dry Squad, stationed in Eureka, used the contraband they confiscated to enliven their red-hot parties on the shores of Sophie Lake under the cloak of night, or else they celebrated noisily at their homes in town. They knew how to throw a bash, how to get swacked...

Papa's bootlegging days were terminated abruptly. Late one October night a cheerful guy came in and asked, "Harry, you got a drink for a thirsty hunter?" "Sure", Papa said agreeably, reached under the counter and poured a glass, but the instant he held it out to the man he knew he was in trouble. "Harry, you're under arrest. I've been trying for a long time to nab you." Papa was fined and spent thirty days in the Missoula Jail and, while doing time, became fast friends with the Sheriff and his wife. They kept him in cigars, played cards with him, chatted with him, and saw to it that he had a daily newspaper. (Papa was lost without a newspaper.) His treatment was royal. Once the Sheriff's wife asked him, "Harry, what's a nice young man like you doing here?" Harry's Place was the most prosperous and popular of the pool halls in Eureka at that time.

The Truth Or Not

Some federal dry agents were not reliable and truthful. *The session of district court being held at Libby at which the liquor cases were being tried blew up suddenly Monday when Judge Pomeroy ordered the case he was trying dismissed, discharged the jury panel, and ordered the remaining cases continued until the March term. In addition, the Judge ordered witnesses for the defense in one of the cases arrested for perjury, which will make additional cases for trial when a jury is again called. Four cases were tried and in each case the defendant was acquitted by the jury. It is reported that the evidence of the defendants tended to show the four men of the dry squad used questionable methods in securing evidence and they were roundly scored by the attorneys for the defense for their alleged attempts in inducing people to break the law for the sake of securing evidence. It was evident that the jury drawn did not 'intend to' convict on the kind of evidence submitted, and although it is only hearsay, we doubt if many juries would convict on the kind of evidence, it is said was submitted.* [1-15-25] Further review of newspapers showed another postponement, and nothing was found after that.

It was a heartening story for many Eureka residents in 1925 when one of the stool pigeons who was in Eureka the year before was arrested in Helena for being drunk and received a large fine.

Stryker-Radnor-Olney: A Place To Get Caught

Not surprisingly, one of the favorite stretches of road where federal agents loved to catch rumrunners was the Stryker-Radnor-Olney area where there were long sections with no side roads. One of the biggest hauls (almost 700,000 dollars in today's money) occurred there. Although the story is interesting even more so is the men involved.

Col. Charles L. Sheridan, assisted by Border Patrolmen Daily Bailey and Frank Coombs and assisted by the local (Flathead) sheriff's force, had the biggest catch of rumrunners ever taken in this part of the country when they drew in their dragnet in the wee small hours Sunday morning, when they took into custody eight men alleged to be rumrunners at Radnor. An inventory showed eight automobiles and eight drivers. The cars and the men were brought in about six o'clock and the cars were taken to the Main Street Motors garage for safe keeping, while the eight men were taken to jail. The eight cars were loaded ...with 12,000 quarts of Canadian liquor, valued at $40,000.

They appeared before U. S. Commissioner Eugene McCarthy Sunday morning. Three of the young men were from this part of the country; W. E. Baricklow is from the North Fork country, while George Farrer and Clyde Leonard are from Eureka. The other boys were fine looking young fellows, all well comfortably dressed, not one of them appearing to be over 25. They were required to put up bonds of 500 dollars each or go to jail, like a bunch of university boys who had been caught in a prohibited prank and were

ready to take the consequence with a smile. It was intimated that they were in the employ of someone higher up and were attracted to the venture by the high price offered for their dangerous mission. They were all bound over to appear in the United States district court at Great Falls.

The cars, which included one Cadillac, two Hudsons, two Overlands and three Fords, were all confiscated by the government, and they will be sold later. It is estimated that the wholesale price of the liquor captured would run up better than $16,000, the retail price being several times that amount around 40,000 dollars.

Monday morning the liquor was taken out to the city dump and the bottles smashed. It is said that several people visited the dump after the wreck and that some of the bottles failed to break. These were gathered up and carried away. One man was reported to have taken a large bucket and emptied the bottom part of the bottles, where there remained some of the liquor, into the bucket. It is said he recovered a couple of gallons of liquor by this method, these stories however, have not been verified, but likely have some foundation.

The loss to whomever foots the bills will run up to more than $25,000 it is estimated. There were something like 12,000 bottles of various kinds of liquor smashed at the city dump, which represented the outlay of a small fortune by somebody. It was thought that the five strangers taken in with the cars were from Butte. They were not armed and made no resistance when surrounded by the officers, taking their arrest good naturedly and made no effort to get away. It is said that there were two more cars ahead of the

eight taken that passed through this city late Saturday night and made good their escape. [Western News 1-9-1930 and 1-16-1930 reprinted from the Daily Inter Lake]

List of persons arrested and property seized at 1:50AM January 5, 1930 at a point on the Whitefish-Eureka road about 25 miles west of Whitefish.

    Customs Officers present.
      Col. Chas. L. Sheridan, Collector of Customs, Great Falls
      Daniel.P. Bailey, Customs Agent, Havre, Montana.
      Frank.D.Coombs, Senior Customs Patrol Inspector, Eureka, Mont.
      Joe Danens, Customs Patrol Inspector, Cut Bank, Montana.
      Roy H. Weatherly, Customs Patrol Inspector, Cut Bank, Mont
      Harry E. McGee, Customs Patrol Inspector, Malta, Montana
      Wm.E. Drake, Customs Patrol Inspector, Chinook, Montana.
      Earl R. Welliver, Eureka Customs Patrol Inspector, Eureka, Mont.

Herb Davis, Rexford, Montana.
1 Hudson coach, Engine #309666, Montana license #17802 for 1929.
12 quarts of cognac fifths.
24 pints of Sauterine
72 quarts of rye whiskey, U.D.L. Imperial.
120 quarts of rye whiskey, Corby's, Imperial.
122 quarts of scotch whiskey, Haigs Dimple, fifths.
12 quarts of wine, cherry.
60 quarts of scotch whiskey, Grants, fifths.
48 quarts of scotch whiskey, Sandy McDougal, fifths.

Jack Wilson, Missoula, Montana.
1 ford tudor sedan, Engine No. A1349176, 1929 Mont. license No. 114214
96 quarts scotch whiskey, Haigs Dimple, fifths.
48 quarts scotch whiskey, Sandy McDougal, fifths.
120 quarts rye whiskey, U.D.L., Imperial.
Stanley Delosh, Verdon Hotel, Spokane, Washington.
1 Oldsmobile Coupe, engine No. 167718, 1929 Washington license #272595.
60 quarts rye whiskey, Corbys, fifths.
108 quarts rye whiskey, Corbys, Imperial.
12 quarts Benedictine liquer.
24 pints of bourbon whiskey, old Colonel.
24 quarts, scotch whiskey, Vat. "69". Imperials.

W.E. Barricklow, Kalispell, Montana.
1 Ford coupe, engine No. A1052775. 1929 Mont. license No, 107965.
52 quarts scotch whiskey, Johnny Walker, fifths.
90 quarts cognac, fifths.
12 quarts cocktails, martini.
138 quarts rye whiskey, Corbys, Imperial.
18 quarts wine, vermouth.
27 quarts scotch whiskey, old Highland, fifths.
36 quarts rye whiskey, Monogram, fifths.
15 quarts scotch whiskey Sterling, fifths.
1 quart gin, Gilbeys, fifths.
1 Min. gin, Gilbeys.

```
C.A. Leonard, Eureka, Montana.
  1 Hudson sedan, engine No. 390698, serial No. 691381, 1929 Mont. Lic.
#21532.
19 sax Fernie Beer (24 quarts to sack)

Michael McDugan, Eureka, Montana.
  1 Cadillac touring Car, model 59, eng. #59n65, 1929 Mont. Lic. #11931.
19 sax Fernie Beer. (24 quarts to sack)

Jack Blair, Tait Hotel, Butte, MOntana.
  1 Ford Coupe, engine No. A2204590, 1929 Mont. License No. 65181.
24 quarts Vermouth wine.
35 pints Bourbon whiskey, old colonel.
198 quarts rye whiskey, Monogram, fifths.
12 quarts sherry wine.
12 quarts bourbon whiskey, old colonel, Imperial.
288 Min. rye whiskey, Monogram.

Virgil Farrar, Eureka, Montana.
  1 Oakland coach, engine No. L237744, 1929 Mont. Lic. 107595.
60 quarts of scotch whiskey, Five Scotts, fifths.
48 quarts of scotch whiskey, spreyside, fifths.
12 quarts of rye whiskey, Monogram, fifths.
36 quarts of bourbon whiskey, Pebbleford.
24 quarts of champaigne wine.
12 quarts of sherry wine.
12 quarts of scotch whiskey, Johnny Walker, Fifths.
12 quarts of cognac.
72 pints of Bourbon whiskey, old Colonel.
```

Notice in this official report the drivers hometowns and other facts that differ from newspaper accounts.

A True Amateur

In the same section of road a rumrunner was caught and arrested; one must feel sorry for him. Victor Asqueta, who claims to be an Idaho sheepherder by profession, was arrested near Radnor at 2 o'clock Friday morning and his new Cadillac car and 25 cases of whiskey were seized. The arrest was made by Federal officers who lodged the prisoner in the county jail and took the car and its cargo on to Missoula. Direct information was filed, charging him with transporting liquor. He entered a plea of guilty and was sentenced by Judge Pomeroy to serve 60 days in the county jail and pay a fine of $300. Asqueta told the officers that he has always been a sheepherder, at which occupation he had saved $2000 which he decided to invest in a bootlegging enterprise as [it would be] furnishing quicker and larger profits. He bought his car and proceeded to Canada, bought his first cargo, and was nabbed before he had an opportunity to market a single case. "I had $2,000 when I left Boise;" Asqueta said, "now she's all gone." [Eureka Journal 6-12-24]

Lucky It Was A Thumb

Tillie Butts and Bill Hume, Jr related the story of their father's short rumrunning days. In 1931 their 17 year old father decided to make a little money when asked by a man to drive a car to Butte. Together they went to Roosville and crossed the border where a car was waiting for them. Inside were containers filled with booze. They drove to Butte, parked the car in a destinated spot and left. Someone must have been watching as a driver picked them up and drove them back to Eureka. The event was well planned because at neither Roosville nor Butte did they meet anyone other than the driver who said nothing. On the second trip Bill Hume drove by himself and again it went without a hitch.

The third trip did not! He and the older man, who rode with him the first trip, again went to the border and began their journey to Butte. In a narrow spot near Olney, they suddenly met two cars nose to nose blocking the road and men with guns at the ready. His partner said "get down and don't move. They are federal agents." Bill of course did so without question. The driver hit the ditch and got around the cars. Bullets started flying and striking the brand new 1931 Model A touring car.

The driver reached up to adjust the mirror when a bullet took off his middle finger. Reaching a point near where Stillwater River was next to the road they pulled over, slipped the containers in the water and were doing first aid on his finger when the dry squad men pulled up. When asked why they ran they said they thought they were hijackers or highway robbers. The dry squad men didn't believe them, but found no evidence when they searched the car, so they departed. Bill and his partner pulled the containers from the river and continued to Butte. Bill decided he could make money another way!

Was It The Same Jane?

The seizure of a Hudson coach with an Idaho license at Gateway on May 22 was reported to Colonel Charles L. Sheridan, collector of customs for this district Thursday. The car was loaded with four sacks of gin, one sack of whisky, one sack of Scotch and six sacks of British Columbia beer. The seizure was made by officers of the immigration patrol and after investigation turned over to the customs office. The car was driven by Jane Newton of the Victoria Hotel Spokane. The woman was arrested, and the car and booze will be confiscated. [Great Falls Tribune 5-27-1927] This was the same name a woman gave agents in the article "Most Rumrunners Escape". Wonder if it was the same woman!

He's All Man

Sheriff Frank Baney's badge

The man charged with enforcing Prohibition in Lincoln County was Frank Baney. He was one of the most fearless and beloved law enforcement officers in Montana history. He became the first sheriff of the newly created Lincoln County (carved out of Flathead County in 1909). Except for a few years as a deputy state game warden, he served continuously until his retirement in 1946. The *Libby Herald* called him a "fearless, honest, likable official (who was) gaining a reputation (statewide) of being a model sheriff," and urged his reelection "because he is right as a golden guinea." The *Eureka Journal* described him as "brave, fearless, efficient, (but) always obliging and courteous."

Burl Holgren wrote Baney's biography and described him in four words "He's all man." "Baney's complete familiarity with his environment — the forests and mountains of the area — helped him in what sometimes seemed to the "man in the street" an almost superhuman intelligence in tracking criminals." Frank Baney was shot by two criminals in 1920. The bullet narrowly missed his heart, but he managed to squeeze off four shots, wounding one of the two criminals. They were later caught and after a long recovery Baney continued as sheriff for almost thirty more years. Most of the time, however, he avoided gunplay and was usually successful in talking would-be gunfighters out of shooting. Most of Baney's prisoners came to trust him and even like him. He had a lively sense of humor and enjoyed pranks. The book tells many of the amusing and lighthearted incidents in which the sheriff was involved. He was a dedicated lawman, but he was first a human being."

For four years Frank Baney has been sheriff of Lincoln County. When the record is finally made up it will be found that no stain mars his official life. He has been one of the very best peace officers in Montana. Fearless as a lion, he never shrank from any duty: yet he never paraded his power or made offensive use of his authority. He didn't regard his office as a pushover: ever he was found ready to serve with unflinching fidelity and unfailing courtesy the public whose servant he regarded himself to be. There is nothing of the braggart or bully or four-flusher about Frank Baney. He is simply a quiet level-headed, honest and fearless man of plain, practical, decent purposes. — Excerpt from the Western News December 24, 1914. Twenty five years later on August 24, 1939, the Western News republished this endorsement of Frank Baney under the headline "We Still Feel the Same Way".

How popular was Frank Baney? In his elections he carried all three Lincoln County towns of Troy, Libby, and Eureka, a feat seldom accomplished by any candidate.

Sheriff Baney As An Enforcer

With Lincoln County the center of rumrunning and bootlegging, Sheriff Frank Baney was a busy man. His first alcohol bust occurred less than a month into Montana Prohibition. He was offered a drink by a big Swede and Baney sampled the drink. It was the real thing! Both the vender and liquor were escorted to jail. [Eureka Journal 1-30-1919] Gunplay with local moonshiners was a rare event. Maybe that is why on one memorable occasion Baney, acting on a tip, drove to the Fisher River country with his wife, Victoria, along. A still had been located above Jennings and Baney was out to get the moonshiner. Baney cautioned her to stay in the car when he stopped. Victoria sat and waited for what seemed like hours and hours. Suddenly she heard several shots. Terrified, she leaped out of the car and raced through the woods in the direction of the shooting. She saw Baney standing beside a broken spouting still. A strange man stood close, white-faced and obviously upset. "I heard the shooting and knew there was trouble. Why didn't you come back and let me know that you were all right?" Baney indicated the copper boiler and tubing, "I couldn't bust this thing up—so I had to shoot it open."

They took the stranger, one of the still's operators, into town. The other moonshiner had vamoosed when he heard Baney coming and in his rush had left his shoes. The next day Baney went back and caught him too.

The Eureka Journal took note of many still busts. In March 1926 an article mentions Baney took down three in one week. The first was a 50 gallon still near Jennings,

Montana. Later that week he found a 90 gallon still just north of Jennings. He finished off the week with a small still on a ranch near Fortine. [Eureka Journal 3-25-1926] The headlines were colorful, "Baney Makes a Big Haul." "Sheriff Halts Moonshining." "Baney Indulges in Favorite Past Time." The headlines could go on and on. A quick survey of arrests over one visit to the Tobacco Valley show a man was nabbed while bringing a load of beer from Canada, three railroad men at Rexford were arrested on the charge of illegal possession of liquor, two prominent men in Fortine were arrested for selling liquor, two women in Eureka who were rooming-house operators were also arrested for selling booze. Another article mentioned Baney destroyed five stills in the Troy area in August 1921. Sheriff Frank Baney and local lawmen like Libby Chief of Police Ferd Bockman seemed to wage a continuous, if losing battle with the local brewers.

The most complete "distillery" Baney found was naturally on Pinkham Creek, ten miles from Eureka. There was no trail or road leading to it. Baney had simply nosed it out like a red-bone hound. He stated afterward that he didn't see how they had moved their equipment into such a remote, wooded place. It was said that the owners were two recent newcomers from Virginia—but they caught on fast. They had gone to an extensive bit of work in setting up their plant. It was located on a side hill near a spring. They had brought the spring water to the still by galvanized iron pipes, which furnished a gravity cooking system. A large pot built up on rocks was the outer compartment of a double-cooker arrangement. Resting in it was a copper globe in which the mash was dropped and from the globe a copper pipe ran down through barrels fed with cold spring water, and the finished "likker" dripped clear and strong into glass jars below. The owners—tipped off no doubt—had fled and were not captured. Baney couldn't find any moonshine—but located five barrels of mash—and broke up the skillfully contrived distillery... [Utter]

"Stop! Stop In The Name Of The Law!"

While most rumrunners did not carry guns a few did. Sometimes it was a rifle if there were two rumrunners. One would break out the back window and try to put a bullet into the radiator of a pursuing car. On the other hand, lawmen frequently used their guns to stop the smugglers autos. Their target was the tires. At least once the dry squad employed

Sheriff Baney with his pistol, he was known as a very good shot.

the same practice as rumrunners in Eastern Montana. When Mike Cuffe of Eureka was looking for a car to purchase, he answered an ad. A lady had not one, but a pair of rumrunner cars. Both had a bullet hole in their radiators. The car's owner related how the rumrunners travelled together, but the dry squad could never catch them until a sharpshooter's bullets did the trick with the radiators.

On one trip to the border Baney was after a Eureka man and was familiar with his car. *Baney drove his own jalopy to a narrow place in the road near the "69" ranch (about halfway between Eureka and the border), and pulled up across it, blocking passage from either way. When he heard a car coming and it was the one he was waiting for, he hailed it and ordered the driver to stop. The driver ignored him and shot past, pouring it on. Baney climbed hastily into his own car and began a hot pursuit. He stuck his head out and yelled, "Stop! Stop in the name of the law!"* Four Eureka residents, two men and two women, had a good lead. Bottles began flying out the windows. but Sheriff Frank Baney "stepped on it" and within a mile was alongside the fleeing car shouting at them to stop. *He shot off one of the hub caps and a wheel spoke splintered. This got results and the driver finally pulled over and surrendered. Baney took the four occupants of the car into town and went back to collect the evidence.* The sheriff gathered up "12 quarts of good whiskey in a gunny sack," some broken, others intact. [Eureka Journal 9-2-1920 and Harmon] The Eureka paper added "four parties were in the car, but out of respect for the parents of one and in light of later developments, we refrain from publishing their names at this time."

The Dry Squad Stops The Sheriff

While coming from Libby recently by auto with Sheriff and Mrs. Baney, the editor [Oscar Wolf] had the experience of witnessing the search of a car by government officials. As the car neared the city limits it was flagged down by a stranger, who informed us that he was a government officer. Mr. Baney submitted to the search gracefully and with a smile, not even informing the officer who he was. Some thought it a huge joke that the major and the sheriff were stopped by enforcement officers and Cub Reporter Mooney said it was the first time two "Dutchmen" were ever held up without a bottle. However, some of Mr. Baney's political opponents are making capital out of it and are untruthfully stating that a bottle was found in his car and that he was let off because he was the sheriff. [Eureka Journal 10-28-26]

The Dry Squad Found Nothing

As mentioned, the most notorious moonshine area was the Pinkham Creek area. *It was said the Pinkham Creek boys were from West Virginia and at least one, Josh Hatfield, was a relative of the infamous Hatfields. They knew how to make moonshine and did so openly. They protected their stills fiercely and it was said even Sheriff Baney left them alone. [Frederickson]. Sid Workman told this story. When I was about 5 years of age my father had a small canvas teepee. He used it for camping and hunting trips. One morning after my older brothers had gone to school he said "Sid, how would you like to have the teepee for a*

playhouse?". Well, that suited me fine. To my amazement he dug a hole about 4' deep in the ground where the teepee was to be pitched. Then he rolled a barrel of moonshine mash out there and carefully lowered it in the hole, covered it with short pieces of board and canvas then a layer of dirt. Next, he gathered some scraps of wood and built a fire. This fire did away with the signs of fresh digging. Next came the teepee pitched directly over the cache. Well, I moved in and was instructed to tell no one what I was living over. In the next day or two we were visited by the revenue officers who made a thorough search for moonshine or the makings.

Nothing was uncovered and we all felt secure again. The barrel of mash was dug up and returned to its own place to finish brewing. I learned later that our county sheriff, Mr. Frank Baney, often times would alert the moonshiners, if possible, of the coming of the revenuers. In those days White Lightning was a good part of the income for the homesteaders. [Utter]

Can that instance be reconciled with the above stories with Madeline Utter's description of Sheriff Baney? Did he really avoid dealing with some moonshiners up Pinkham? No, the newspaper articles mention still busts on Spring Creek, Cooks Run, and several others only mentioned as Pinkham Creek. There may be at least two possibilities for this difference. First that after 1926 Baney was not responsible for enforcement of Prohibition and second, maybe he avoided the stills of long time Pinkham families, but that conflicts with a story that John Doble told. John related how Baney came to the home of a Pinkham Creek moonshiner and as he was destroying his still asked him if he would quit the moonshine business if he got him a job, which Baney did and the man quit the moonshine business. One geographical feature on today's maps is a reminder of the exciting days of Prohibition. STILL CREEK, a stream which flows into Pinkham Creek, is named after a moonshine still found in the area during Prohibition days.

Montana Victims Of Prohibition Enforcement

Unfortunately, with guns being fired accidents happened. *It takes but a short time for the government to order the transfer of one of its agents accused of murder from state to federal court, and a much shorter time for the accused to be freed on the ground that he was in the performance of a public duty when he willfully shot into an auto, building or some other place and killed an innocent man.* [Facts About Prohibition Number 7 Billings Gazette 10-19-1930].

The Washington Herald did a survey in 1929 trying to identify the number of victims of the Prohibition Enforcement in the United States. Deaths were counted only when law enforcement was involved. The paper identified 1360 people including four children under 12 years of age killed nationally.

For Montana they identified three Enforcement Officers killed and five civilians. The County Sheriff of Big Horn County and a special officer of US Indian Service were killed in an ambush. The shooter was later killed by a posse on October 28, 1926. A Lewiston policeman was killed by an alleged bootlegger, December 1, 1925.

The five civilians were a man in the Musselshell County Jail who died from an alleged lack of medical care, following an arrest on a liquor charge. A miner killed by two Prohibition Agents Fletcher and Jones, June 10, 1929. Another alleged bootlegger killed by two Special Officers in Rosebud County and another person killed in Rosebud County with no details given. [Omaha Sunday Bee, 12-15-1929]

The fifth civilian listed on the survey was one that occurred near Glacier National Park. Omar Dillman and a companion, Elmer Allegree, were driving near the park when they encountered Monroe and two other federal officers. The young men did not stop fearing the agents were robbers. The agent suspecting Dillman and a companion of being liquor runners from the Canadian border shot. The car continued a short distance and stopped. Dillman was found dead leaning on the steering wheel, shot in the head. No liquor was found in the car. Glacier county officials charged Monroe with manslaughter and he was convicted and sentenced to from one to two years in prison. His conviction was affirmed by the high court… [Helena Independent 1-10-29] In August, seven months later, his conviction was commuted by the court.

Ferd Bockman photo Montana Law Enforcement Museum

The paper mentioned only verified victims were identified, but the number is low. At least one more law officer and civilian were shot and killed in Lincoln County. Libby Chief of Police Ferd Bockman was killed by a bootlegger while trying to make an arrest in April 1924. A posse later found the shooter and after a gun battle as he was dying, he refused to give his name. The funeral of the beloved lawman was one of the largest ever in Libby. The identity of the killer was unknown for fifty years, until he was later identified as George Menees York of Tennessee when a relative requested copies of the newspaper detailing the shooting. [Brockman]

One other officer was killed in Montana after the newspaper survey. On July 22, 1933, brief months before national prohibition became a memory, Paul A. Read, a federal agent, was shot to death by C. W. Cates between the Missoula County jail and the courthouse. Cates was sentenced to hang, and the scaffold was prepared, but after several reprieves the sentence was commuted to life imprisonment. Cates was paroled in March 1956. Don't you wonder how many others may have died during Prohibition enforcement?

Although not in a confrontation, one Gateway Agent was killed during Prohibition. During the evening of April 4, 1925, Patrol Inspectors Joseph P. Riley and William A. Blundell were patrolling in a government-owned car about 1 1/2 miles from Eureka, Montana, when the tie rod broke, causing the automobile to leave the roadway. The vehicle continued over a high bank and then into a ditch and turned over, pinning Patrol Inspector Riley under the steering wheel. Patrol Inspector Blundell was not seriously injured. Patrol Inspector Riley sustained a fractured cervical vertebra and a spinal cord injury. He was conveyed to the Eureka Hospital. The attending physician advised that

Patrol Inspector Riley's condition was so serious that facilities were not available for providing proper attention at Eureka and he recommended moving the patient to Spokane, Washington. On April 5, Patrol Inspector Riley was transported by train to Spokane, where he was placed in the Sacred Heart Hospital. He succumbed at 6 a.m. on April 6, 1925, from respiratory paralysis. [US Customs IN Memorian] Joe Riley was the first customs officer to die on the Northern border.

Joe Riley

The Danger Of Being A Prohibition Officer

While standing on a bluff between Gateway and Roosville a federal Prohibition officer narrowly escaped death when fired upon by some unidentified person. The officer heard the report of a rifle and heard a bullet whizz by his head. No one was in sight. The enforcement officer was not chasing anyone. It is assumed by officials that a bootlegger hid in the brush on the Canadian side and tried to murder the man who he probably knew was a federal officer. The officer was never identified.

One who was identified was the lucky or unlucky federal officer, Jack Curtis. His name struck terror to those who made their living by violating the liquor laws of the state and nation. Five times the target for bullets from the guns of desperate moonshine makers and rum runners, four times victim of those bullets. The first time Jack Curtis was wounded was in April 1922, not far from Arlee, when he was fired on from ambush. The bullet lodged in the back of his left shoulder.

His second experience four months later in September near the Canadian border was like a gun fight from the old west. Officer Curtis told the story. When we met the whiskey-runner's car Smith got out and stopped him, we were not expecting to find any whiskey as he was going toward Canada but thought best to search the car to make sure. Smith showed him his badge and told him who he was.

"You got a warrant?" Curtis said the whiskey-runner asked. "No, we don't use warrants," replied Smith. "Then, boys, you have got me. I have got a load," and the runner smiled and appeared willing to climb down out of the machine. Smith, thinking he was coming out of the door near him put his hand on it to open it for the runner.

When he looked up, a shotgun was thrust into his face. Smith is said to have turned an appealing look toward Curtis and dropped just as the automatic shotgun rained a shower of buckshot over his head. Both Curtis and the runner believed Smith was dead. Following the flash of the shotgun, Jack's pistol barked, and a bullet struck the whiskey-runner in his left shoulder, turning him around facing Curtis.

A duel followed, pistol against shotgun, buckshot penetrating Jack's cap, grazing his scalp and tearing a hole in one of the shoulders of his coat. When he had emptied his pistol, he reached for the shotgun in the car and leaped out. "Drop that gun," Curtis is said to have commanded. The whiskey-runner raised his gun with difficulty and fired. Curtis returned the fire, two shots striking the whiskey-runner, who crawled into the thick brush.

Curtis returned to the car for ammunition and during his absence the whiskey-runner made his escape in the brush, crawling over to the Canadian side where he was lost from sight. The officers searched the thicket on the American side of the border but found no trace of the man. "When I looked into the muzzle of that shotgun, I thought it was all over," said Smith. I glanced at Jack. He was standing up in my car and just as the whiskey-runner shot I dropped, and I saw Jack open fire." The car was seized and searched. In it were found 13 sacks of bottled goods. The car was confiscated." [Eureka Journal 9-21-1922]

In May 1923, Jack was fired on while standing near a building at Pablo. The bullets hit the building about two feet from where he was standing. It was dark and no trace of his assailant could be found.

In June 1923 was shot in the back again near Arlee when searching for a still. He was going up a narrow canyon hunting for a still. Two deputy sheriffs were with him, about 150 yards away. The bullet came from a rifle about 100 yards from Mr. Curtis. While in the hospital in Missoula he was interview. "I was shot just as I slipped on rock trail leading to a moonshiner's outfit about 10 or 12 miles up the Jocko River from Arlee," Mr. Curtis indicated that he had told the whole story and there was nothing more to say. "Your business is mighty dangerous, and one would think you would get out of it," said the interviewer. Mr. Curtis smiled. "I am not frightened as yet," he replied, "and an officer must take what he gets." That was his only comment. He recovered and continued his job.

There were several attempts on Jack's life later. An attempt was made to run him over on the highway between Ronan and St. Ignatius in May of 1932. Another time unidentified assailants, driving in a large sedan, fired upon Curtis at Post creek, ten miles south of Ronan. The attack was made in the dark when Curtis was examining the engine of his car. He was fired upon twice that night and one of the bullets from a revolver struck his arm, while a shotgun charge tore away the leg of his trousers, but the shot did not penetrate the flesh. The shock knocked him down. Jack survived all these attempts on his life only to die in a car crash in May 1935.

Ambush By Dry Agents At Roosville

Sometimes it was the civilians who were in danger! In 1927 two controversial incidents occurred. When an auto did not stop at the border, which was common in those days. Agents claimed they hollered at the occupants of the car to stop, and they claim to not have heard. Agent Roy Mitchell fired several shots assuming they were rumrunners, and the passenger was wounded. He was a sales manager for an oil refinery company and he and his companion were on the way home from a meeting. The man was quickly taken to the Eureka hospital and survived. No booze was found in the car. A warrant was later issued for the officer, and he posted a bond of 1500 dollars. [Eureka Journal 7-1-1926]

The second incident was *to shoot first and investigate afterwards. This was evidently the scheme of the two dry enforcement officers who Monday night shot up the new Nash coupe owned by D. W. Beirley, but the two skulking cow-*

ards did not then 'have the decency' or nerve to investigate or, aid and succor their victim or victims as the case might have been, but sneaked off into the darkness without making any demands or disclosing their identity, according to the occupants of the car, who, without their knowledge, had a very narrow escape from death. Mr. Beirley, accompanied by Harold Mosby and two lady companions, had motored into Canada Monday evening on the Roosville road. Returning sometime after dark... they heard a noise and the car swerving to one side, the driver, Mr. Beirley stopped, saying that a tire had blown out.

They proceeded to use the spare. This also was deflated and after several attempts to inflate it, gave the matter up and came in on the flat tire Mr. Beirley thought had blown out. On opening his garage the next morning, Mr. Beirley was astounded to see that the body of his beautiful new car had been punctured in one place and marred in three or four other places by buckshot. The front tire that had given out had also been punctured as had the spare, which he had unsuccessfully attempted to inflate. Upon further investigation one of the spent shot was found on the floor of the car. This evidently was the one that had punctured the car close to the driver's head.

A full investigation was then begun by Mr. Beirley and

Stop and report sign [Tobacco Valley Museum photo]

from drivers of other cars that were stopped by the officers stationed there on duty that night the identity of the men who were on duty was discovered. One car had been stopped a short distance beyond where the shooting occurred and while Mr. Beirley was endeavoring to fix his tire, and these officers questioned the parties as to whose car was down the road (meaning Beirley's) Another car or two passed about that time and Mr. Beirley seems to have plenty of witnesses and evidence, both circumstantial and real, that his car and the occupants were shot at without warning by "dry squad" men on duty.

Sheriff Baney was called up from Libby and came up Tuesday evening to investigate. In company with Officer Armstrong, who had stationed the two men on guard there the night before, visited the scene. It is said that it is admitted that the shot recovered is the same as is used in the guns of the "dry squad." Yesterday afternoon Pat Gould and Olay Berg, members of the "dry squad", were arrested by Sheriff Baney on a charge of assault with a deadly weapon. A hearing was set for Friday morning at 10 o'clock and the defendants were released on bond. This is the second affair of this nature within the year, the other being the shooting last fall by an overzealous youth, Roy Mitchell, under somewhat similar circumstances. The Beirley affair seems even less excusable as it is stated no demand was made for the car to stop, the shot being fired from ambush, and then the officers never made an appearance. Employment of gun men of this kind is doing the dry cause no good, and it is no wonder the sentiment is swinging toward a modification…
[Eureka Journal 6-2-1927]

Punishment For Prohibition Crimes

Originally a list of towns and cities in Montana where violations occurred was compiled. It became apparent that every isolated country abode, town and city had events and after one years' worth of research of the papers there were more arrests, deaths, fines, and bonds than you could shake a stick at as the sayings goes.

Here is a unique one from Olney; a man was arrested by customs border patrol for having an empty bottle with Canadian labels, he was taken to Eureka to a Customs officer and fined two dollars to pay for a duty on the bottle. [Eureka Journal 5-31-1928]

Eurekan Calix Dugas was charged with selling liquor to a minor. His case was dismissed as the witnesses disappeared. Disappearing witnesses was a common occurrence as many did not want to stick around for a trial scheduled months later. Dugas was loved by everyone from tots to the aged. He was a fiddler at dances, town marshal and later a taxi driver. No doubt this offence occurred when he was a saloon keeper, a place he was seldom seen sober. [Eureka Journal 4-12-1928]

A Speakeasy in Great Falls had bond set at 1000 dollars (Eureka Journal 5-19-26) and a Missoula man who had a still had a bail set at 1000 dollars (Eureka Journal 1-20-21). This demonstrates how fines for still owners were much higher than for other offenders except speakeasies who could easily afford a stiff fine.

Moonshiners And Rumrunners In Jail

Edmund Farly, after six years of being a rumrunner, was finally arrested. His trial was set for six months later and in between he continued rumrunning until his trial. He was fined 2000 dollars and sentenced to six months in jail. He was immediately made a trustee and had complete freedom during the day to wander the halls. He met murderers, safe crackers and lazy husbands (nonsupport charges) in jail, he could visit inmates through the cell bars. He wasn't even forced to be dry. Seized liquor was poured into a bathtub and he always seemed to be near when it was time to dump the booze. He would slip a bottle for himself in his pockets and even one small bottle capable of slipping through the bars for the cellmate next to the bathtub who witnessed his thievery. Another ingenious trustee knew the pipe from the bathtub went into the kitchen and he devised a way to divert it for his own use. Now is a good time to mention that where county or city hall stored "evidence" seized in raids it was common for some of it to go down the gullets of employees rather than down the drain!

Just as Fahey became a trustee in his jail, Frank Baney too made some violators trustees who were given a wide range of freedom. Beryl Holgren for her book interviewed his wife. At first Victoria felt that all prisoners were dangerous, and she was glad of the heavily locked doors that separated her from them. She especially feared bootleggers and moonshiners, as a kind of wild breed apart from the rest of the lawbreakers. Gradually, as she came to observe and understand them, she lost her fear and learned to feel that they were among the world's unfortunates.

One moonshiner had a fine family but couldn't seem to resist the temptation of making a batch of "moon" occasionally, and of course was arrested. While serving his time he became a trustee and was allowed to go to the shed and carry in wood for the jail stove. Victoria's son Duke, about three years old, would follow him faithfully because he liked the old moonshiner and liked to visit with him. He called the old fellow "Arpen." One day after "Arpen" was back in the cell, Victoria missed Duke. She asked the jailer if he'd seen Duke. "He might have gone out when Martin got in the wood," replied the jailer. Victoria hunted outside without success, then decided to go and find out if "Arpen" knew where Duke was. Duke was in jail sitting on "Arpen's" lap with a cribbage board on his knees. The jailer hadn't seen Duke when he locked the old trustee up. "What are you doing?" asked Victoria, who had been worried. "Playing sixteen-two with Arpen," replied Duke, proudly holding a handful of cards. From then on, his old friend had a new name. Duke always called him "Sixteen-two."

One harmless old moonshiner, a trustee whose sentence was about up, was allowed to work outside. When Baney left on a case he told Victoria, "At six o'clock, see that he's locked up." When it came time to lock him up, Victoria called him, and he went into his cell. She made a few unsuccessful attempts to hold the big, heavy padlock in place as she turned the key. But she couldn't manage to hold the padlock—it kept slipping. Finally the prisoner after watching her failure, said, "Here, let me try." She gave him the key and from the inside of the cell he locked the door on himself, then handed her the key.

Montana Quits Enforcement

Montana with many rumrunners and moonshiners, decided in 1922 to increase the penalty for possession of booze. What was a fine as low as 25 dollars with an option of no jail time was changed to a mandatory 200 dollar fine with a jail time of not less than 60 days. Judges and juries were not always compliant. A Helena Judge removed 'twelve good and true men' from the jury panel after they found a bootlegger not guilty even after he admitted his guilt and three agents avowed, they purchased it from him. After dismissing the jury, the Judge fined the bootlegger 300 dollars for possession. [Eureka Journal 2-2-28]

As the expense and time involved in enforcing Prohibition as well as the decrease of the population believing in the positive effects of the same, Montana people turned against Prohibition. A referendum was put on the ballet for the fall 1926 election to repeal Montana liquor laws, opining that cities and towns could enforce their own dry laws. The referendum passed and Montana became the first state in the union to abolish its own Prohibition. The Lincoln County vote was close, 1172 for repeal and 1133 against repealing the laws.

Most cities and towns did not have any laws. The sheriff's office of Big Horn County reported a great deal of criticism for not taking a more active part in the enforcement of liquor law violations. In 1928 they asked the Montana Attorney General, L. A. Foot, for an opinion regarding the subject: "No sheriff nor any of his deputies has any authority to arrest a violator of the Prohibition act, interfere with the running of a still, or take part in suppression of the rum traffic, except that a federal officer may be given aid on request, but no mileage or emoluments may be received for the aid by a county officer so aiding." According to the letter the board of county commissioners were also prohibited from allowing mileage to the sheriff or his deputies for assisting a federal officer in discharge of his duties. (Eureka Journal 8-2-1928) Lincoln County too did not have any laws on the books, there were no more reports in the papers about Sheriff Baney having any still discoveries or rum-runner stops after 1926. A review of district court records before 1927 shows two out of three cases or even maybe three out of four cases were for manufacturing, transporting, selling or possessing liquor.

After the state of Montana declined to further enforce Prohibition, the city of Whitefish passed an ordinance making it illegal to sell liquor within three miles of the city limits. Being arrested for bootlegging became a matter of a court appearance and a small fine. Bootlegging made money for the city, but it wasn't exactly a crime. Ed Paddon paid a $25 fine in March 1927 for selling liquor. David Bergstrom paid the same amount when caught making it. Judge Van Waggenen's court tried liquor cases with total fines of $1650 that year. Raids by Federal Dry Squads and aided by local police, rounded up offenders and sent them to the local courts. Even many local drys disliked the procedure and sympathized with those caught. Editor Moss editorialized on May 31, 1927: "Let's enforce the laws, even Prohibition, but in an orderly, sensible way." The situation became even more confused in 1928, with periodic raids, more court appearances, and fines, and finally a sticky moment when a self-named "undercover man," G. L. (Scarface) Williams, sued Mayor Poorbaugh for $102 as he said he had not been paid for work performed "snooping" to find liquor violators. [*Stump Town to Ski Town*].

Federals Agents Continue The Losing Battle

Federal operations continued in the fight to end bootlegging, moonshining, and rumrunning. In Montana 10 field agents and 24 customs agents continued the battle. In July, 24 more officers were assigned to the Montana and Idaho borders to replace Montana lawmen.

Sometimes federal customs agents were shorthanded... J. C. Armstrong, border inspector at Gateway, following the seizure of a Buick touring car on June 20, permitted the driver to act as chauffeur while Mr. Armstrong rode in the front seat with him. The rumrunner increased the speed until they reached a place in the road which runs along a high embankment and then he jumped over. Armstrong grabbed the steering wheel, but before he could stop the car, the driver had escaped into the underbrush. [Great Falls Tribune 6-29-1927]

In 1926 Sheridan said his agents "seized so many high powered cars that now they seize battered, secondhand wrecks that have little value." Newspaper accounts tell a different story that many expensive autos were still being captured by agents. Federal agents continued to make many rumrunner stops confiscating six cars in June 1927 alone and 14 by Christmas in the Eureka area that were in the paper, there may have been more. Charles Sheridan gave an official count for October 1927 when agents confiscated 10 cars and 2298 quarts of liquor in Montana for that month.

Seized autos were sold at auction. When local police like Frank Baney seized an auto, it was sold at auctions in Libby or Eureka. Money after expenses was given to schools. Cars grabbed by Federal agents were taken to Missoula or Great Falls for auction and probably that money went to Federal coffers.

The End Was Coming

This article was published in the Missoulian in 1929 with the headline *Rum-Running from Canada Unprofitable*. Many times when they (rumrunners) are halted on the roads at night, and that is when most of the whiskey-runners travel, the rumrunner knows when he is caught. Usually, he deserts his car and takes to the brush. Seldom do the federal officers go far in pursuit of the man and thus give him a chance to again get back to his car and escape. They get the car and the load, and although the owner has escaped, he has suffered a serious financial blow. "The odds are against the rumrunner when he is operating… Often a whiskey-runner gets a good start, only to be run down miles away from the border by federal men who seldom miss their judgment in a whiskey car." [Again, the facts really don't support this article as expensive cars were still being seized and rumrunners still escaped the clutches of the law.]

First Roosville Customs Building. Notice land behind the station, rumrunners could only use the land between this station and Gateway. Gary Montgomery photo

Roosville opened a new border station in March 1927. In June it was announced that the port at Roosville, having been created as a permanent port of entering vehicles of every description, it is necessary and compulsory for every person going into Canada or coming from Canada to immediately report to the U S. Customs office. Persons returning from Canada shall not go beyond the custom house or the residence of the deputy collector without first reporting, nor shall they discharge any passenger before reporting. The provisions of the Tariff Act of 1922 will be strictly enforced in the future, and anyone coming from Canada or having gone to Canada without a permit and is apprehended by the Border Patrol or other Federal officer will be subject to

$100 fine. [Eureka Journal 6-9-27] Art Fleming reported that after this move to Roosville he was the only customs officer in Gateway.

Further attempt to stop smuggling occurred in November when U. S. Custom officials constructed a gate across the Roosville road at the international boundary and locked it between the hours of 5 p.m. and 8 a.m. *It is understood that during the daylight hours of from 8 a.m. to 5 p.m. there will be an officer present to clear cars and passengers, but during the other hours it will be necessary for those wishing to cross to go to Gateway or violate the law by using some of the various trails. While it may curb the liquor traffic to some extent, it will be a great inconvenience to the people of Lower B. C., and this section, and the new rule is not regarded with any degree of pleasure by those affected.* [Eureka Journal 11-25-27]

Can You Believe The Government's Poisoning Plan?

Early on, even before national Prohibition, authorities recognized there was a problem with denatured alcohol. Denatured alcohol has additives to make it poisonous, bad-tasting, foul-smelling, or nauseating to discourage its recreational consumption. Since 1906 toxic chemicals were included in industrial alcohols to prevent people from drinking them. In the first month of Montana Prohibition authorities did not understand that the denatured alcohol was being redistilled into hopefully drinking alcohol. *Denatured alcohol, with its amiable nature restored by some*

mysterious process, is causing the police to worry over the enforcement or the prohibition laws, according to Commissioner J. H. Tilsley. Drug stores of late are receiving dozens of calls a day for denatured alcohol. Alcohol customers go away with the liquid, which is poisonous in the shape in which it is sold, take the stuff home and, in a few hours appear on the street drunk. Just what is done to take out the poison and make the alcohol drinkable is not known. The police have made several arrests lately of persons who were intoxicated from this source according to the commissioner. "Something must be done to stop the practice," declared Mr. Tilsley. "But I do not know what it will be. The drug store owners are willing to cooperate with the authorities, I am certain, but legislation is needed to end the trouble. At present the police are powerless, as there are no laws prohibiting the sale of denatured alcohol." [Eureka Journal from the Spokane Chronicle 1-9-19]

As mentioned, 30,000 people died during Prohibition from poisoned alcohol. Historical facts can sometimes be stranger than fiction. Even claims that at first sound unbelievable can be rooted in truth. The fact is one third of those people died because of a government poisoned alcohol. Frustrated that people continued to consume so much alcohol even after it was banned, federal officials decided to try a different tactic. In simple terms they went on an approach that many people considered unethical.

By 1926 the government figured bootleggers were distilling 60 million gallons of denatured alcohol each year. So the government ordered industrial distillers to make their industrial alcohols more deadly. Specifically, twice as deadly! The long list of approved poisons included such deadly ones like Chloroform, Carbolic acid, Brucine (similar to strychnine), and Formaldehyde (the major content of embalming fluid). The government had to approve the poison formulas. These additional chemicals were hard to remove by redistilling.

The government never directly poisoned drinking alcohol. The idea was to scare people into giving up illicit drinking. The government defended its action. A leading official was blunt. "The great mass of Americans does not drink liquor. There are two fringes of society who are hunting for "booze." They are the so-called upper crust and the down-and-out in the slums. They are dying off fast from poison "hooch." If America can be made sober and temperate in 50 years a good job will have been done."

The Anti-Saloon League agreed, "The Government is under no obligation to furnish the people with alcohol that is drinkable when the Constitution prohibits it. The person who drinks this industrial alcohol commits a deliberate suicide. 'To root out a bad habit costs many lives and long years of effort." Some accused lawmakers opposed to the poisoning plan of being in cahoots with criminals and argued that bootleggers and their law-breaking alcoholic customers deserved no sympathy.

The poisonings outraged many people. One senator called it "legalized murder." Another said, "Only one possessing the instincts of a wild beast would desire to kill or make blind the man who takes a drink of liquor, even if he purchased it from one violating the Prohibition statutes." As one of its most outspoken opponents, Charles Norris, the chief medical examiner of New York City during the 1920s, liked to say, it is "our national experiment in extermination."

But the government would not stop. Addison K. Lusk, federal director of Prohibition enforcement in Montana had this attitude. *The moonshiner is a most undesirable citizen. He is usually of foreign extraction the experience of enforcement officers has shown. He is usually a low type of man, and as a rule, if rumrunning becomes unprofitable, he will resort to bank robbery or other crime. In patronizing the moonshiners and bootlegger you are harboring a menace to society which you and your family will eventually pay for either indirectly or directly.* With people like Mr. Lusk in control, it is no wonder that the program of poisoning never ended.

It is safe to say during Prohibition, an official sense of higher purpose kept the poisoning program in place. As the Chicago Tribune editorialized in 1927: "Normally, no American government would engage in such business. ... It is only in the curious fanaticism of Prohibition that any means, however barbarous, are considered justified."

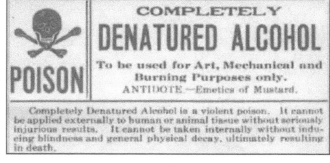

Denatured bottle label

The poisoning continued until the end of Prohibition. That was seven years later. By then, over 10,000 Americans died from the government's poisoning program.

Now You Can Drink Beer

When the depression hit, governments at all levels became "thirsty" for the taxes they used to make off the sale of alcohol. Politicians saw people were still drinking, except that all the profit was going to law breakers instead of them. Prohibition was an important issue during the U.S. presidential election of 1928, but Herbert Hoover's win over Al Smith ensured that what Hoover called an "experiment, noble in motive" would continue. As the Great Depression continued to grind on, however, it became increasingly clear that the Volstead Act was unenforceable. The public was tired and clambered for a change. In March 1933, shortly after taking office, Pres. Franklin D. Roosevelt signed the

No Speakeasy needed! First Beer After Prohibition in Butte April 8. 1933 photo Butte-Silver Bow Archives.

Cullen-Harrison Act, which amended the Volstead Act and permitted the manufacturing and sale of low-alcohol beer and wines (up to 3.2 percent alcohol by volume). Basically, the amended Volstead Act allowed people to have a beer or two while they waited for the 21st Amendment to be ratified.

Brewing Companies were ecstatic! In April 1933, August A. Busch, Sr. was given a gift by his sons of a six-horse Clydesdale team hitched to a wagon to commemorate the repeal of prohibition of beer. Realizing the marketing potential of a horse-drawn beer wagon, the company arranged to have a second six-horse Clydesdale team sent to New York to mark the event. They delivered a case of Budweiser to former Governor Alfred Smith, who had been instrumental in fighting prohibition. They proceeded on a tour witnessed by thousands, cumulating with another crate of beer delivered to President Roosevelt at the White House.

An Amendment Needed To Repeal An Amendment

Just as it took time for laws to be enacted after the passage of the 18th Amendment in 1919, winding down those laws also took some time. Congress proposed the 21st Amendment in February 1933, and took the unusual method of calling for state conventions to vote by December 5, 1934, on the amendment instead of submitting it to state legislatures.

On December 5, 1933, Pennsylvania, Ohio, and Utah had conventions that voted to repeal Prohibition. This made the total of 36 states who wanted to end Prohibition—the three-quarters majority required by the Constitution. The ratification of the 21st Amendment marked the end of federal laws to bar the manufacture, transportation, and sale of intoxicating liquors. The 21st Amendment returned the control of liquor laws back to the states who could legally bar alcohol sales across an entire state or let towns and counties decide to stay "wet" or "dry."

Two states (North and South Carolina) rejected the 21st Amendment before December 5, so the vote was not unanimous. Eight states didn't meet before December 5 and didn't vote one way or the other on the 21st Amendment: Georgia, Kansas, Louisiana, Mississippi, Nebraska, North Dakota, Oklahoma, and South Dakota. Maine and Montana were not among either group. Maine ratified the amendment the day after the amendment was ratified and Prohibition ended.

Montana Was In No Hurry!

Montana, though wet by legislative action since 1927, in August 1934 joined other states of the nation in ratifying the twenty-first amendment. By a delegate vote of 45 to 4, a state constitutional convention went through the motion of ratification, largely as a matter of keeping the record clear… While entitled to 79 delegates, the convention was far short of that number due to the failure of many counties to name them. Others used only a portion of their actual allocated voting strength. The convention, held in the house chamber at the capitol, was purely an uneventful meeting… (once

the business of naming a chairman and secretary was over) Attorney General Enor K Matson advised the delegates on the manner of procedure and Chief Justice L. L. Callaway administered the oath. The rest was simple and brief. Two committees, one on credentials, another on the resolution of ratification, were formed, and when the latter reported late in the afternoon, the vote was immediately taken... [Billings Gazette August 7, 1934] Montana was the last state to approve the amendment as the article notes "largely as a matter of keeping the record clear."

Results Of Prohibition

Prohibition destroyed the fifth largest industry in the United States which was the production, distribution, and sale of alcoholic beverages. Previously there had been licensing and strict regulation of legal alcohol producers and sellers. Prohibition led to police corruption, which corroded public trust in law enforcement. Further, it led to jails and courts being full of people who were caught with alcohol.

Crime, poverty, violence, marital abuse, industrial injuries, sickness, and premature death would all go down were the main arguments for Prohibition. None of the promises come true! Crime increased as organized criminals quickly seized on the opportunity to exploit the new lucrative criminal racket of speakeasies and clubs and welcomed women in as patrons. In fact, organized crime in America exploded. Al Capone, leader of the Chicago Outfit, made an estimated $60 million a year supplying illegal beer and hard liquor to thousands of speakeasies he controlled in the late 1920s.

Gangsters gained control of the liquor trade with murders, gun fights, and bribes, which are portrayed in popular histories, films, books, and other media. Rumrunners and moonshiners were mostly ordinary people.

Prohibition made many problems worse and created new problems. Innocent bystanders were killed. Murder increased sharply. Drinking bootleg alcohol paralyzed, blinded, or killed many people that was increased by the federal government's regulations. Cash-strapped restaurants and bars shut their doors since they could no longer make a profit from liquor sales. Revenues shrank for many states that had previously relied on liquor taxes to fund roads, schools, and other public benefits. Enforcement proved impossible to achieve. Murders, gun fights, and profits were far less in Montana.

Rumrunners Caches Found Years Later

Although not recently, caches from moonshiners and rumrunners would be found for years after Prohibition in the Tobacco Valley. Sometimes to hide the evidence rumrunners would hide booze in a hole or dugout basement from a deserted house. Some cases were found during construction excavations years later. Ed Clark recalled his family's storage. "That reminds me of some of that good old rhubarb wine and dandelion wine. Dad would bury it in the dirt in the cellar… I found some Canadian whiskey there once. It seemed like whenever we needed meat from the cellar, I never had to go get it and sometimes everything else was done before I got to cook the meat. Everybody was happy though." [Ed Clark]

The Cost of Prohibition In Dollars

When Prohibition ended, a book was published called the *Price of Prohibition*. No one disputed the stated cost! For the estimated recovery of 46 million dollars, the cost was one billion dollars spent trying to enforce Prohibition. [Eureka Mirror 8-16-32]

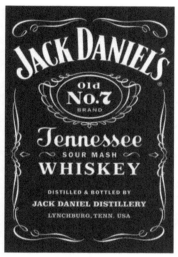

Jack Daniel's label

Some Still Have Prohibition Today

Even after the repeal of Prohibition, some states maintained a ban on alcohol within their own borders. Kansas and Oklahoma remained dry until 1948 and 1959, respectively, and Mississippi remained alcohol free until 1966—a full 33 years after the passage of the 21st Amendment. To this day, 10 states still contain counties where alcohol sales are prohibited outright. The nearest dry county to Montana is Oglala Lakota County in South Dakota (which is located entirely within the Pine Ridge Indian Reservation).

Another interesting fact: Jack Daniel's is one of the most famous whiskeys in the world. The distillery is located in Moore County, Tennessee which is one of the state's many dry counties. While it is legal for the company to distill the product within the county, it is illegal to purchase it there. However, a state law has provided one exception: the distillery may sell one commemorative product sample.

NASCAR

To end the story of Prohibition, a cheerful story. One result of Prohibition was it led to one of the most popular sporting events. To elude federal Prohibition agents, sheriffs and cops on the road daring "runners" needed sharp driving skills to speed and maneuver along dirt, gravel, single-lane, and occasionally, paved roads often after dark and at times with their headlights turned off. Those were the men who became the first car racers leading to National Association for Stock Car Auto Racing, or NASCAR, in 1947.

Even before Prohibition came to an end in 1933, racing high-performance cars became a popular pastime among the "runners" in the South. They raced each other's cars on weekend afternoons out in the country on makeshift dirt tracks.

Prior to the formation of NASCAR, in 1946 and 1947 beach races were held, both were won by former rumrunner Red Bryon who won the first Nascar race in 1948. Photo NASCAR Archives.

How similar bootleggers were to stock car racers. Booze runners looked for good mechanics who knew how to make their engines run faster and handle better than police vehicles. Fahey wrote, "The rum smuggler put his cars through mechanical tests as tough as those devised by test drivers," he wrote. "Tires were put to the severest possible tests. Heavy loads hauled over the toughest of roads often at reckless speeds, kept the rubber on your car always under the utmost strain. Therefore, the rum smuggler at all times used the best tires that could be bought. In fact, several companies developed tires especially for the rum-running trade. Many a runner served time in jail simply because his rubber failed him at some critical moment." Sounds like a race car driver and crew!

The legacy of the Prohibition runner went beyond casual backwoods racing in 1936, when the city of Daytona, Florida, held the first organized stock car race as a promotion. It lost money, but a Prohibition-era mechanic named Bill France, who placed fifth in the race, was determined to find a way to organize stock car racing. It took him more than a decade, but NASCAR's organization set a single set of rules for racetracks and formalized the sport. The first NASCAR race was held in Daytona on February 15, 1948. The winner, in a modified Ford, was Red Byron, a former moonshine runner! Fahey dropped out of the runner's racket after an arrest and six-month jail sentence in the mid-'20s and did not end up as a racer.

The Final

The Eureka Journal, which is the source of most of these articles, ceased publication in March of 1929. The editor, Oscar Wolfe, decided to leave Eureka. I was able to fill the four year void that created by adding family stories and articles from the two newspaper internet sources.

Enforcement of Prohibition continued, but Americans were tiring of the stories that dominated the headlines for the last ten years. Even Al Capone was in jail by 1929. People became more concerned with the economy following the stock-market crash that occurred in October. By 1930 the Depression was in full swing, and the world was suffering. But it was still three years before Prohibition ended. During that time rumrunning continued.

Sources

For this booklet a lot of my initial research was on the internet for national items and background information on Prohibition, but many of the Montana stories that make this booklet so interesting are from Montana newspapers. Some newspapers quotes have been changed to make them easier to read and/or to understand. Two newspaper sites were valuable. A pay site https://www.newspapers.com and a free site http://montananewspapers.org. Most other entries are from the Eureka Journal.

Davis, Kenneth H., *My Life Story*, Unpublished Autobiography, Fahey, Edmund, *Rum Road to Spokane*, University of Montana Publications, Missoula, Montana 1972

Flanagan, Darris, "Carrie Nation visited Eureka," *Eureka, Montana Standing the Test of Time*, Self-published, Eureka, Montana, 2019

Fraley, John, *Wild Rivers Pioneers*, Big Mountain Publications, Whitefish Montana, 2008Frederickson, Mary, "Bootleggers in and Through Lincoln County," *Pages from the Past*, Institute of the Arts Writers Group, Libby, Montana, 1989

Harmon, Jim, "Sheriff Frank Baney Served Lincoln County with Courage and Compassion," harmonhistoriesl.com, Missoula Current, Missoula, Montana March 29, 2021

Holgren, Beryl, *Frank Baney Forty Years a Montana Law Enforcer*, Vintage Press, New York, New York 1965 Holgren, Beryl. *Looking Back Laughing*, unpublished, Kalispell, Montana 1991

Johnson, Olga, *Tobacco Plains Country*, Pioneers of the Tobacco Plains Country, Eureka, Montana 1950

Montgomery, Gary, "A Conversation with John Morgan," The Trail, Winter 2013 #107, Trego, Montana 2013

Montgomery, Gary, *Still Whiskey from Sid Workman*, Old Time Recipes from the Historic Tobacco Plains Journal, Eureka, Montana 1995

Moore, Steven T., Bootlegging and the Borderlands: Canadians, Americans, and the Prohibition Era Northwest, College of William & Mary - Arts & Sciences, Williamsburg, Virginia

Otto, Teresa, Nuts to the Noble Experiment Montana Cussed Women Bootleggers, Distinctly Montana, February 15, 2023

Schafer, Betty and Engeiter, Mable, *Stump Town to Ski Town*, Whitefish Library Association, Whitefish, Montana 1973

Shea, Marie, Gateway, Newgate, and Roosville *Early Flathead and Tobacco Plains*, Self-Published, Eureka, Montana 1977

Shields, Mark, *Liquor is Now Sold Openly Over Bars at Butte*, Spokane Chronicle, Spokane, Washington, 10-24-1922.

Sonju, Jean, "The Bockman Family," *Pages from the Past*, Institute of the Arts Writers Group, Libby, Montana, 1989

Utter, Madeline, *Pinkham Pioneers*, Stoneydale Press, Stevensville, Montana 2006

Wilson, Gary A., *Honky-Tonk Town Havre's Bootlegging Days*, Montana Magazine, Helena, Montana 1985

Oral Histories in Tobacco Valley Museum: Irene Abby, Ed Clark, Emmett Quirk and Earl and Helen Hansberry

Additional stories from John Stoken, Jeff Gruber, Tilley and Bill Hume, Jr., John Ellis, Mike Marvel, John Leonard, Pat Doble, JoAn and Mike Cuffe

https://www.cbp.gov/about/in-memoriam
US Customs and Border Protection, IN Memorian

https://www.odmp.org/search/browse/montana
Officer Down Memorial Page Montana Line of Duty Deaths